# Start Leading, Stop Managing

Winning in the C-Suite

Michael Bruno

EPIC AUTHOR
PUBLISHING

www.EpicAuthor.com

Epic Author Publishing | support@epic.media | www.EpicAuthor.com

ISBN (Paperback): 978-1-947276-78-9
ISBN (eBook): 978-1-947276-77-2

Printed in the United States of America.

For permissions, inquiries, or bulk orders, please contact: **mbruno730@gmail.com**

**Get Your Book Bonuses**

**Scan to Access**

# Contents

# Preface

Leadership is not about managing processes, it is about inspiring people, setting a vision, and driving impactful changes. In today's fast-paced, complex business world, the distinction between leading and managing is more critical than ever. *Start Leading, Stop Managing: Winning in the C-Suite* is a wake-up call for executives and aspiring leaders who want to break free from traditional management constraints and rise to the true calling of leadership.

As a former executive myself and across more than 30 years as an executive and leadership advisor, I have seen firsthand that the best leaders are not just skilled at oversight and execution; they are visionaries who challenge the status quo, navigate uncertainty with confidence, and empower those around them to achieve extraordinary results. This book is a road map to mastering that level of leadership.

The following chapters are designed to equip you with the essential skills needed to excel in the C-suite. From Strategic Thinking and Visionary Mindset to Decision-Making and Innovative Thinking, you will learn how to develop a leadership style that drives transformation and long-term success.

But leadership is more than strategy—it is people. The sections on Emotional Intelligence, Executive Presence, Persuasiveness, and Resilience will help you refine your ability to inspire and connect with others, making you not just a boss, but a leader people choose to follow.

In the ever-evolving corporate landscape, adaptability is key. The insights into Crisis Management, Agility, and Learning Agility will prepare you to lead in times of uncertainty, ensuring that your organization not only survives but thrives. Meanwhile, Financial Management, Negotiation, and Data-Driven Decision Making will empower you with the analytical prowess required to steer businesses toward sustained profitability and growth.

What truly sets this book apart is its comprehensive approach. Beyond execution and strategy, leadership in the modern era requires a deep understanding of Stakeholder Management, Cultural Intelligence, Board Governance, and Mergers and Acquisitions. These are the competencies that distinguish great leaders from good managers.

If you are ready to transition from a results-driven manager to a transformative leader, this book is for you. The insights contained within these pages will help you refine your leadership style, enhance your influence, and unlock new levels of success in the C-suite.

Leadership is not a title—it is a responsibility. Now is the time to stop managing and start leading.

Welcome to your journey of leadership excellence.

Michael Bruno

# Introduction

The path to the C-suite is both exhilarating and demanding. The pinnacle of corporate leadership is not just about ambition, but about the skills and characteristics that define those who succeed at the highest levels of business. While many aspire to titles like Chief Executive Officer (CEO), Chief Financial Officer (CFO), Chief Operating Officer (COO), Chief Human Resources Officer (CHRO), Chief Information Officer (CIO), or Chief Marketing Officer (CMO), few understand what it takes to excel in these roles.

*Start Leading, Stop Managing: Winning in the C-Suite* is designed to provide an in-depth exploration of the critical elements that shape an executive's career. Through extensive research and years of professional observation, I have identified twenty-nine essential skills and defining characteristics that significantly influence an individual's ability to thrive in the C-suite. These are more than checkboxes; they're foundational pillars upon which leadership success is built.

## Why This Book Matters

A quarter of the way through the 21st century, business landscapes are transforming faster than ever before. The digital revolution, globalization, regulatory changes, and shifting workforce dynamics have transformed the business landscape. What made an executive successful a decade ago may not be enough today. Leadership in the modern era demands adaptability, resilience, and a deep understanding of both business strategy and human behavior.

Yet, despite the wealth of information available on leadership, there is often a lack of structured guidance that blends technical proficiency with the intangible personal attributes that set outstanding executives apart from average managers. This book aims to bridge that gap by offering a comprehensive framework that professionals at all career stages can use to evaluate their strengths, address their weaknesses, and cultivate a well-rounded executive presence.

If you are an aspiring executive seeking to climb the corporate ladder, this book will serve as your road map to identifying and honing the skills and characteristics necessary for leadership success. If you are already in an executive role, *Start Leading, Stop Managing* will challenge you to refine your approach, develop a deeper level of self-awareness, and enhance your ability to lead with impact.

## 29 Skills and Characteristics That Make a Difference

At the heart of this book lies a two-part framework. One part focuses on the hard skills required to lead an organization and the other centers on the personal characteristics that define exceptional leadership.

These twenty-nine skills and characteristics cover a broad spectrum of competencies, including:

- **Strategic Thinking:** The ability to look ahead, anticipate trends and position an organization for long-term success.

- **Financial Acumen:** Understanding financial statements, budgeting, and forecasting.

- **Operational Excellence:** Ensuring efficiency in business processes and systems.

- **Crisis Management:** Leading effectively during times of uncertainty and disruption.

- **Data-Driven Decision Making:** Leveraging analytics and insights for informed leadership.

Equally important are **Characteristics**, which include:

- **Emotional Intelligence:** The capacity to understand and manage emotions effectively.

- **Resilience:** The ability to recover from setbacks and maintain a steady course.
- **Integrity:** Prioritizing honesty and ethical responsibility.
- **Humility:** A willingness to listen, learn, and accept feedback.
- **Visionary Thinking:** The capacity to inspire and articulate a compelling future.

While some leaders naturally possess a strong blend of these skills and characteristics, others must consciously develop them. Regardless of where you stand today, recognizing the importance of this balance is the first step toward long-term success.

## What You Will Gain From This Book

Throughout the following chapters, you will gain:

- a clear understanding of the competencies required for executive success.
- practical insights into how to cultivate these skills in real-world scenarios.
- strategies for self-assessment and continuous professional development.
- lessons from real-life executives who have demonstrated these qualities.

Success in the C-suite is not simply about intelligence or ambition; it is about cultivating a holistic leadership approach. By systematically addressing both skill development and personal growth, you can position yourself as a formidable executive capable of navigating complex business environments with confidence and expertise.

## A Final Thought Before We Begin

Many professionals believe that reaching the C-suite is the ultimate career milestone. However, the reality is that achieving the title is only the beginning of your journey. Executives must continuously evolve, refine their approach, and expand their knowledge to remain effective leaders. The most successful business leaders are lifelong learners, unafraid to challenge themselves and adapt to the changing tides of industry and innovation.

Whether you are just starting your journey or are an established leader seeking to refine your skills, this book will serve as a critical resource in your professional development. As you read, take time to reflect on each skill and characteristic. Identify areas where you excel and those that require further attention. By doing so, you will not only enhance your executive potential but also contribute to building a more dynamic, resilient, and forward-thinking organization.

Let us begin this journey together and explore what it truly takes to succeed in the C-suite.

# 1

# See What Others Miss

*Strategic Clarity, Foresight, and Innovation Help You Lead Beyond the Obvious*

## Section I: Strategic Thinking

### Zoom Out Before You Zoom In

Strategic thinking is one of the most critical competencies for executives in the C-suite. It enables leaders to make informed, forward-looking decisions that shape an organization's long-term success. In a rapidly changing business environment where technological disruptions, economic shifts, and geopolitical challenges constantly evolve, executives must possess the foresight to navigate uncertainty and drive sustainable growth.

### What Is Strategic Thinking?

Strategic thinking refers to the ability to anticipate future trends, identify emerging opportunities, and make decisions that align with an organization's overarching mission and objectives. It is not just about long-term planning but also about adaptability, creativity, and calculated risk-taking. Effective strategic thinking enables C-suite executives to lead proactively rather than reactively.

Key components of strategic thinking include:

- **Vision and Foresight:** Seeing beyond immediate challenges to anticipate future opportunities.
- **Analytical Skills:** Evaluating complex data to inform decision-making.
- **Innovation and Creativity:** Developing novel approaches to competitive challenges.
- **Agility and Adaptability:** Pivoting quickly in response to unforeseen changes.
- **Risk Management:** Balancing opportunities and threats in decision-making.

## The Role of Strategic Thinking in the C-Suite

Executives on the C-suite are responsible for steering the organization toward its goals. Whether the CEO, CFO, COO, or CHRO, each leader must integrate strategic thinking into their leadership approach. Here are some ways different C-suite roles must think strategically:

### Chief Executive Officer (CEO)

The CEO is the ultimate decision-maker, responsible for defining the company's strategic vision. Strategic thinking at this level involves:

- setting long-term goals and aligning the organization's efforts toward them.
- recognizing emerging trends and positioning the company to capitalize on them.
- making bold decisions, such as acquisitions, expansions, or shifts in business models.

### Chief Financial Officer (CFO)

A CFO must think strategically about financial planning and resource allocation. This includes:

- ensuring financial sustainability by balancing growth investments and risk mitigation.
- identifying cost-saving opportunities without sacrificing long-term success.
- navigating economic fluctuations while maintaining profitability.

**Chief Operating Officer (COO)**

For a COO, strategic thinking revolves around efficiency and execution. Key aspects include:

- optimizing internal processes to improve productivity and profitability.
- aligning operational strategies with business goals.
- managing supply chain disruptions and technological advancements.

**Chief Marketing Officer (CMO)**

A CMO applies strategic thinking by:

- understanding market trends and consumer behaviors to shape brand positioning.
- leveraging data analytics to optimize marketing campaigns.
- identifying growth opportunities through product innovation or market expansion.

**Chief Human Resources Officer (CHRO)**

For a CHRO, strategic thinking means:

- ensuring the workforce aligns with the company's future needs.

- leading cultural and organizational changes to foster innovation and agility.

- developing talent pipelines to sustain leadership succession.

## Strategic Thinking in Action: Notable CEO Examples

### ***Jeff Bezos, Amazon***

Jeff Bezos, the founder and former CEO of Amazon, is a prime example of strategic thinking in the C-suite. Bezos built Amazon into one of the world's most valuable companies by focusing on long-term goals rather than short-term gains.

Key strategic decisions:

- **Customer-centric innovation:** Bezos prioritized customer satisfaction, introducing innovations like Amazon Prime, which increased customer loyalty.

- **Diversification:** Under his leadership, Amazon expanded into cloud computing (AWS), entertainment (Prime Video), and artificial intelligence (Alexa).

- **Risk-taking:** Bezos consistently reinvested profits into future growth areas, even at the cost of immediate financial returns.

***Satya Nadella, Microsoft***

In his first 10 years as CEO of Microsoft, Satya Nadella transformed the company by focusing on cloud computing and fostering a growth mindset within the organization.

Key strategic initiatives:

- **Shift to cloud computing:** Nadella pivoted Microsoft's focus from Windows to Azure, making the company a leader in cloud services.

- **Cultural reinvention:** He changed Microsoft's culture to encourage collaboration and learning, ensuring employees were open to innovation.

- **Acquisitions and expansions:** Strategic acquisitions such as LinkedIn and GitHub expanded Microsoft's influence in the professional and developer communities.

## Developing Strategic Thinking Skills in the C-Suite

Strategic thinking is a skill that can be cultivated. Here's how executives can develop and refine their strategic mindset:

**1. Stay informed.**

- Read industry reports, market analyses, and thought leadership articles.

- Attend forums and engage with other business leaders.

- Keep a pulse on technological advancements and global economic trends.

**2. Foster learning throughout the organization.**

- Encourage continuous learning within the company.
- Create an environment where employees feel empowered to innovate.
- Promote cross-departmental collaboration to gain diverse perspectives.

**3. Encourage scenario planning.**

- Develop contingency plans for potential risks.
- Use data analytics to forecast business outcomes.
- Regularly review and adjust strategies based on real-time feedback.

**4. Seek mentorship and advisory boards.**

- Leverage experienced mentors or executive coaches.
- Form an advisory board with industry experts to provide strategic guidance.

- Engage in peer networking to exchange insights with other leaders.

**5. Embrace innovation and experimentation.**

- Encourage calculated risk-taking within the organization.
- Allocate resources for research and development to explore new business opportunities.
- Adopt a fail-fast mentality where failures are learning opportunities.

## Challenges to Strategic Thinking in the C-Suite

While strategic thinking is essential, some issues can hinder the ability to plan effectively. Common obstacles include:

- **Short-term pressure:** The demand for quarterly earnings can limit long-term vision.
- **Risk aversion:** Fear of failure may prevent bold, transformative decisions.
- **Siloed thinking:** Lack of cross-functional collaboration can stifle innovation.
- **Information overload:** Filtering vast amounts of data into actionable insights can be overwhelming.

To overcome these challenges, leaders must remain adaptable, prioritize long-term objectives, and build a culture that values strategic decision-making.

## Conclusion

Strategic thinking is a vital competency for C-suite executives, influencing an organization's ability to thrive in a dynamic business landscape. By cultivating a forward-looking mindset, leveraging data-driven insights, and fostering a culture of innovation, executives can drive sustainable growth and maintain a competitive edge.

CEOs like Jeff Bezos and Satya Nadella exemplify how strategic thinking can reshape industries and propel organizations to new heights. For aspiring and current executives, embracing strategic thinking is not just an advantage—it is a necessity for long-term success in the C-suite.

# Section II: Critical Decision-Making for Scaling

## Decide Fast, Own the Outcome

Scaling a company is one of the most challenging and high stakes endeavors a business can undertake. The process demands not only operational adjustments but also strategic foresight, risk assessment, and leadership agility. At the heart of this transformation lies critical decision-making within the C-suite. Executives, particularly CEOs, must navigate market uncertainties, talent acquisition, financial structuring, competitive threats, and innovation demands to ensure sustainable growth.

## The Role of the C-Suite in Scaling a Company

Scaling is distinct from simple business growth. While growth involves increasing revenue at a linear pace, scaling refers to the ability to grow revenue exponentially while keeping costs proportionally lower. C-suite leaders must provide the following to scale successfully:

- **Strategic Planning and Vision:** The leadership team must define a clear road map that aligns with market opportunities and internal capabilities.

- **Operational Efficiency and Processes:** Ensuring that company operations can sustain increased demand without sacrificing quality or efficiency.

- **Talent Acquisition and Culture:** Building a workforce that can support expansion without diluting company values.

- **Financial and Risk Management:** Balancing investment and cost efficiency to avoid over-leveraging while maximizing returns.

- **Innovation and Adaptation:** Staying ahead of competitors by embracing innovative technologies, business models, and customer expectations.

Each of these domains requires leaders to make high-stakes decisions with incomplete information, making critical thinking and decision-making skills nonnegotiable.

## The Importance of Critical Decision-Making in the C-Suite

One of the most formidable challenges in scaling is uncertainty. C-suite executives must anticipate shifts in market conditions, regulatory changes, and evolving consumer behaviors. Strategic decisions in this context involve evaluating data trends, engaging in scenario planning, and making calculated risks.

For example, Microsoft's core business segments were stagnant when Satya Nadella took over as CEO. His decisive shift toward cloud computing led to the rapid growth of Microsoft Azure, a move that contributed significantly to the company's resurgence as a leader in enterprise solutions.

## Scaling Operations While Maintaining Quality

A company's ability to scale hinges on its operational structure. Poor decision-making in process automation, supply chain management, or service delivery can lead to bottlenecks that stifle growth. Executives must critically assess whether to expand organically, acquire competitors, or forge strategic partnerships to scale efficiently.

For instance, Indra Nooyi, former CEO of PepsiCo, made critical decisions that ensured the company's sustainable growth. She implemented a strategic shift toward healthier product offerings while maintaining PepsiCo's dominance in traditional snack and beverage markets. By investing in R&D and refining supply chain processes, Nooyi ensured that PepsiCo could scale without compromising its commitment to health-conscious consumers.

## Talent Acquisition and Leadership Development

Scaling a company necessitates attracting, retaining, and developing top talent. Poor hiring decisions can lead to inefficiencies and a toxic workplace culture, both of which impede long-term growth.

Jeff Weiner, former CEO of LinkedIn, recognized early on that culture played a pivotal role in scaling the company. Under his leadership, LinkedIn made calculated decisions about hiring, employee engagement, and leadership training. By fostering a people-first culture and maintaining a clear mission-driven approach, Weiner was able to scale LinkedIn's workforce effectively while sustaining an elevated level of innovation and productivity.

## Financial Structuring and Risk Mitigation

Financial decision-making is one of the most delicate aspects of scaling a company. Leaders must determine when to raise capital, how to allocate budgets effectively, and whether to pursue organic growth or strategic acquisitions.

A prime example is Brian Chesky, CEO of Airbnb, who had to make difficult financial decisions during the COVID-19 pandemic. Facing a drastic drop in travel demand, Chesky implemented cost-cutting measures, streamlined operations, and refocused the company's core business on long-term stays and local experiences. These decisions ensured that Airbnb could weather the crisis and emerge stronger once travel demand rebounded.

## Innovation and Competitive Edge

In a rapidly evolving business landscape, companies that fail to innovate will struggle to scale. The C-suite must make calculated decisions about product development, technological investments, and market differentiation.

Consider Mary Barra, CEO of General Motors, who made a bold commitment to produce electric vehicles (EVs) when the automotive industry was still heavily reliant on traditional internal combustion engines. The decisions she made as the lead executive positioned GM as a formidable player in the EV space, ensuring the company would remain competitive in the shifting automotive landscape.

## Characteristics of Effective Decision-Makers in the C-Suite

Given the critical nature of decision-making at the executive level, successful leaders often exhibit the following traits:

- **Analytical Thinking:** The ability to assess vast amounts of data, recognize patterns, and make informed choices.
- **Decisiveness:** The confidence to make tough calls, even in the absence of complete information.
- **Adaptability:** Willingness to pivot strategies in response to emerging challenges.
- **Risk Management:** The foresight to evaluate risks and implement mitigation strategies proactively.
- **Visionary Leadership:** The capacity to inspire teams and align stakeholders around a common objective.

## Conclusion

Scaling a company is a complex process that demands exceptional leadership and decision-making skills. The C-suite, particularly the CEO, must navigate market dynamics, operational challenges, talent needs, financial constraints, and innovation opportunities with strategic clarity.

Leaders like Satya Nadella, Indra Nooyi, Jeff Weiner, Brian Chesky, and Mary Barra exemplify how critical decision-making can drive a company's growth and long-term sustainability. Their ability to assess situations, take calculated risks, and make transformative decisions highlights the indispensable role of strategic thinking in scaling organizations.

As companies prepare for the challenges of expansion, cultivating decision-making acumen within the executive team will be paramount to long-term success. Organizations that prioritize critical thinking in leadership development will be better equipped to navigate the complexities of scaling and emerge as industry leaders in their respective fields.

## Section III: Innovation Matters

### Spot the Future Early: Predict, Then Lead

In the dynamic and competitive business environment, innovative thinking is no longer a luxury. Executives who embrace innovation drive growth, foster resilience, and position their companies at the forefront of their industries. Innovative thinking involves challenging the status quo, embracing disruptive ideas, and fostering a culture of continuous improvement. In this section, we will explore the critical role of innovative thinking in the C-suite, examine its impact on business success, and highlight two prominent CEOs—Elon Musk and Satya Nadella—who embody this mindset.

## The Role of Innovation in the C-Suite

As the highest-ranking executives in a company, C-suite leaders are responsible for setting strategic directions, ensuring operational efficiency, and driving sustainable growth. Innovative thinking in the C-suite is crucial for several reasons:

- **Competitive Advantage:** Businesses that prioritize innovation differentiate themselves in the market and stay ahead of competitors.

- **Adaptability to Change:** Rapid technological advancements and shifting consumer demand require executives to be agile and forward-thinking.

- **Increased Efficiency and Productivity:** Innovation fosters new processes, business models, and technologies that enhance efficiency.

- **Employee Engagement and Culture:** A culture of innovation encourages creativity, employee empowerment, and collaboration.

- **Customer-Centric Growth:** Innovating with a focus on customer needs leads to improved products, services, and experiences.

## Characteristics of an Innovative C-Suite Executive

Innovative leaders in the C-suite exhibit distinct traits that enable them to challenge traditional thinking and drive transformation. These people regularly demonstrate:

- **Visionary Thinking:** They anticipate industry trends and position their companies accordingly.

- **Risk-Taking and Experimentation:** They embrace calculated risks and learn from failures.

- **Open-Mindedness:** They welcome diverse perspectives and current ideas.

- **Collaboration and Empowerment:** They build teams that encourage experimentation and collaboration.

- **Customer-Centric Focus:** They prioritize the necessity of understanding and addressing customer needs.

## Case Studies of Innovative C-Suite Leaders

### ***Elon Musk, Tesla and SpaceX***

Elon Musk, CEO of Tesla and SpaceX, epitomizes innovative thinking in the C-suite. His ability to challenge conventional wisdom, pursue ambitious goals, and create groundbreaking technologies has transformed multiple industries.

- **Revolutionizing the Automotive Industry**: Musk's leadership at Tesla drove the shift toward electric vehicles, making them mainstream. His commitment to sustainable energy and innovative battery technology positioned Tesla as a leader in the EV market.

- **Space Exploration and Reusability**: At SpaceX, Musk pioneered reusable rocket technology, significantly reducing the cost of space travel and advancing the mission of making humans a multi-planetary species.

- **Unconventional Thinking and Risk-Taking**: Musk's accomplishments stemmed from his willingness to take risks. Selling direct to consumers, launching vehicles into space, and investing in AI-driven robotics demonstrated his ability to think beyond industry norms.

### *Satya Nadella, Microsoft*

For more than a decade at Microsoft, Satya Nadella redefined innovation by fostering a growth mindset and prioritizing artificial intelligence, corporate culture, and cloud computing.

- **AI and Digital Transformation**: Microsoft made significant strides in AI, investing in OpenAI and integrating AI into products like Office 365 and Teams.

- **Cultural Reinvention**: Nadella transformed Microsoft's internal culture by encouraging collaboration, learning, and customer obsession, ensuring long-term innovation and success.

- **Embracing Cloud Computing**: Nadella shifted Microsoft's focus from traditional software to cloud-based services, turning Azure into a dominant player in the cloud computing market.

## The Impact of Innovative Thinking in the C-Suite

Innovative thinking at the highest levels of leadership has profound implications for business success:

- **Revenue Growth and Market Expansion**: Companies led by innovative executives often experience exponential growth and enter new markets successfully.

- **Brand Strength and Customer Loyalty**: Pioneering ideas and customer-focused innovation enhance brand reputation and customer trust.

- **Sustainable and Scalable Solutions**: Innovative companies create long-term, scalable solutions that adapt to changing market conditions.

## Conclusion

In the C-suite, innovative thinking is the key to unlocking potential, driving transformation, and ensuring sustainable growth. Leaders like Elon Musk and Satya Nadella exemplify how embracing innovation can revolutionize industries, inspire teams, and create lasting impact. As businesses navigate an increasingly complex and uncertain future, fostering a culture of innovation in the C-suite will remain a strategic imperative for long-term success.

## Section IV: Leading for Results

### Outsmart What Others Try to Outwork

In the corporate world, being results-oriented is a crucial trait for leaders in the C-suite. These executives are responsible for setting strategic goals, optimizing performance, and ensuring sustainable business success. A purposeful leader focuses on measurable outcomes, efficiency, and accountability, ensuring that every decision and initiative contributes to the organization's overall success. Here we'll explore the significance of being purposeful in the C-suite and highlight two CEOs—Jeff Bezos and Mary Barra—who exemplify this approach.

### The Importance of Being Results-Oriented in the C-Suite

Executives in the C-suite must prioritize results in order to drive business growth, maintain competitive advantages, and create value for stakeholders. A results-driven mindset is essential to mastering:

- **Strategic Execution:** A results-oriented approach

ensures that strategies are implemented effectively, aligning business objectives with operational execution.

- **Accountability and Performance Metrics:** Clear goals and KPIs help track progress and ensure that teams stay focused on key deliverables.

- **Customer-Centric Success:** Businesses that emphasize results are more likely to improve customer satisfaction and retention.

- **Operational Efficiency:** Seeking tangible outcomes helps eliminate inefficiencies and optimize resource allocation.

- **Sustainable Growth and Profitability:** Focus on results fosters innovation and long-term financial health.

## Characteristics of a Results-Oriented C-Suite Executive

Leaders who prioritize results exhibit distinct characteristics that enable them to drive business success. Among these traits are:

- **Data-Driven Decision-Making:** Relying on analytics and insights to make informed strategic choices.

- **Clear Goal-Setting:** Establishing ambitious yet achievable goals and ensuring alignment across the organization.

- **Accountability and Ownership:** Holding themselves and their teams responsible for outcomes.
- **Efficiency and Productivity Focus:** Streamlining processes and optimizing operations to maximize output.
- **Resilience and Adaptability:** Navigating challenges with a problem-solving mindset and adjusting strategies as needed.

## Case Studies of Results-Oriented C-Suite Leaders

### ***Jeff Bezos, Amazon***

Jeff Bezos, the founder and former CEO of Amazon, is a prime example of a results-driven leader. His obsession with measurable success and efficiency made Amazon one of the most dominant global companies.

- **Customer-Centric Performance Metrics**: Bezos ensured that every Amazon initiative was tied to customer satisfaction, leading to the creation of services like Prime and AWS (Amazon Web Services).
- **Operational Efficiency and Scalability**: By optimizing logistics, automation, and technology, Bezos built one of the most efficient supply chains in history.
- **Long-Term Thinking with Measurable Milestones**: Despite short-term criticisms, his commitment to

reinvesting profits into innovation paid off through consistent growth and expansion.

***Mary Barra, General Motors***

Mary Barra, CEO of General Motors, exemplified results-oriented leadership by focusing on innovation, efficiency, and financial performance.

- **Electric Vehicle (EV) Revolution**: Barra positioned GM as a leader in the EV market with a clear road map for sustainable growth.

- **Efficiency and Cost Optimization**: Under her leadership, GM streamlined operations, improved profitability, and embraced digital transformation.

- **Accountability and Strategic Execution**: She set clear objectives for GM's transition to an all-electric future, ensuring measurable progress at every stage.

## The Impact of Results-Oriented Thinking in the C-Suite

Results-driven leadership in the C-suite directly influences a company's performance and success:

- **Financial Growth and Stability**: Companies led by results-oriented executives tend to achieve consistent revenue growth and market leadership.

- **Enhanced Organizational Agility**: A focus on

measurable outcomes enables quicker decision-making and adaptation to market shifts.

- **Stronger Stakeholder Trust**: Investors, customers, and employees are more likely to trust leaders who deliver on their promises.

## Conclusion

Being results-oriented in the C-suite is not just a leadership style, it is a fundamental requirement for sustained success. Leaders like Jeff Bezos and Mary Barra demonstrate how a relentless focus on outcomes drives innovation, efficiency, and long-term growth. In an increasingly competitive business landscape, prioritizing results ensures that organizations remain resilient, adaptive, and positioned for continued success.

A leader focused on results may be the catalyst that turns a small-cap company into a mid-cap. Identifying successful executives in mid-cap companies who exemplify a results-oriented leadership style can be challenging due to the varying definitions of mid-cap status, which is typically defined as businesses with market capitalizations between $2 billion and $10 billion. However, here are a few notable leaders:

***Alessio Alionço, Pipefy***

Alessio Alionço, the founder of the San Francisco-based Pipefy who has served as CEO of the AI workflow automation company since its inception in 2015, has been recognized for his strong leadership. Under his guidance, Pipefy achieved significant milestones in its first 10 years, including growing to more than 400 employees and garnering customers around the world. Pipefy's performance reflects Alionço's purposeful approach.

***David Meek, Ipsen***

During his tenure as CEO at Ipsen, a European mid-cap pharmaceutical company, David Meek focused on strategic initiatives that propelled the company's growth. As CEO from 2016-2019, Meek led that growth by acquiring other companies and developing markets in the United States and China. His leadership emphasized open innovation, measurable outcomes, and operational efficiency.

It is important to note that the mid-cap sector is diverse, and leadership effectiveness can vary across industries and regions. For a more comprehensive understanding, consulting industry-specific reports and analyses would provide deeper insights into executives who exemplify a purposeful leadership style in mid-cap companies.

# 2

# Master the Inner Game

*Develop Emotional Intelligence, Resilience, and Authentic Presence for Yourself, First*

## Section I: Relationships Drive Success

### Know Thyself: If You Can't Lead Yourself, No One Will Follow

While technical skills and strategic thinking are essential for executive leadership, the distinguishing factor between good and great C-suite leaders often is emotional intelligence. Emotional intelligence—the ability to recognize, understand, and manage one's own emotions while effectively navigating interpersonal relationships—has become a nonnegotiable trait for executives who aim to drive sustainable success.

### Defining Emotional Intelligence in Leadership

Emotional intelligence, as defined by psychologist Daniel Goleman, consists of five key components:

1. **Self-Awareness:** Recognizing one's emotions and their impact on decisions and interactions.

2. **Self-Regulation:** Controlling impulses and moods to maintain professionalism and composure.

3. **Motivation:** Maintaining a passion for work beyond external rewards.

4. **Empathy:** Understanding and considering others' emotions in decision-making.

5. **Social Skills:** Managing relationships, influencing people, and fostering collaboration.

For C-suite executives, these components are critical because they directly impact leadership effectiveness, organizational culture, and business outcomes.

## Why Emotional Intelligence Is Critical for C-Suite Leaders

- **Improved decision-making:** Executives with high EI assess situations with emotional balance, ensuring decisions are not clouded by impulse or bias. They integrate both analytical reasoning and emotional data to make sound, strategic choices.

- **Stronger leadership and influence:** EI enables executives to inspire and lead with authenticity. By understanding the emotional drivers of their teams, they cultivate trust, loyalty, and motivation, fostering a high-performance culture.

- **Effective communication:** Communication is the core of leadership. Leaders with strong EI tailor their style to different audiences, ensuring clarity, transparency, and alignment within the organization.

- **Crisis management and resilience:** The ability to remain composed under pressure is invaluable. Emotionally intelligent leaders navigate crises with resilience, ensuring stability and reassurance within their teams while making level-headed decisions.

- **Cultivating a positive organizational culture:** A leader's emotional intelligence significantly influences workplace morale, collaboration, and retention. Empathetic leaders foster inclusive and supportive cultures where employees feel valued and engaged.

- **Building strong relationships with stakeholders:** Whether dealing with investors, board members, or employees, emotionally intelligent leaders build strong relationships based on trust and mutual respect. This is particularly crucial in small-cap companies where leadership accessibility and connection to all stakeholders are key to growth.

## Case Studies: Leaders Who Exemplify Emotional Intelligence

***Keri Gohman, Xero Americas***

Keri Gohman, former president at Xero Americas, a leader in the small-business accounting technology space, is known for her empathetic leadership style. During her three-year tenure at Xero Americas, she championed a culture of trust and transparency. Gohman emphasized emotional intelligence in leadership, fostering an environment where employees felt empowered and heard. Her approach to decision-making was deeply rooted in understanding team dynamics and customer needs, allowing Xero to expand its footprint in the U.S. market.

***Brian Halligan, HubSpot***

Although HubSpot has grown beyond a small-cap company, co-founder and former CEO Brian Halligan's leadership in its early years serves as an exemplary case of emotional intelligence in action. Halligan emphasized servant leadership, prioritizing the growth and emotional well-being of employees over organizational output and control. He fostered a company culture based on transparency and authenticity. His empathetic approach to customer relations helped HubSpot create a brand that resonated deeply with small businesses.

## Developing Emotional Intelligence in the C-Suite

Given its importance, how can executives cultivate and strengthen their emotional intelligence?

- **Self-reflection and continuous learning:** Leaders must engage in self-assessment and seek feedback to improve their EI. Executive coaching and leadership development programs can also enhance these skills.

- **Mindfulness and emotional regulation techniques:** Practicing mindfulness, meditation, and stress management techniques can help leaders maintain composure and make emotionally intelligent decisions.

- **Active listening and empathy training:** Leaders who practice active listening ensure understanding before reacting, especially in high-stress situations. They cultivate empathy by seeking to understand different perspectives without judgment and strengthen social skills by giving and receiving feedback gracefully, managing conflict constructively, and building authentic relationships.

- **Leading by example:** Executives set the tone for the organization. By demonstrating emotional intelligence and modeling positive behaviors, they encourage a culture of emotional awareness and interpersonal effectiveness at all levels.

## Conclusion

In an era where leadership demands extend beyond financial acumen and operational efficiency, emotional intelligence has emerged as a defining trait of successful executives. C-suite leaders with high EI navigate complexity with empathy, resilience, and authenticity—qualities that drive sustainable business growth and strong organizational cultures.

Executives like Keri Gohman and Brian Halligan illustrate that emotional intelligence is not merely a soft skill but a strategic advantage. As businesses continue to evolve, the ability to lead with emotional intelligence will remain a key differentiator in executive success.

# Section II: Show Up Like a Leader

## Presence Builds Trust Before You Speak

Executive presence is a critical component of leadership effectiveness, particularly in the C-suite, where leaders are expected to inspire confidence, drive strategic vision, and influence stakeholders. This presence is often described as a blend of gravitas, communication skills, and the ability to project confidence and decisiveness in high-stakes situations. For small- and mid-cap companies, executive presence is especially crucial. These organizations operate in a competitive landscape where strong leadership can separate a company from its peers, attract investors, and help retain top talent.

## Defining Executive Presence

Executive presence is an intangible yet highly recognizable quality that enables leaders to command attention, earn respect, and inspire action. It consists of several key elements:

- **Gravitas:** The ability to project confidence, decisiveness, and emotional intelligence in high-pressure situations. Leaders with gravitas remain composed under stress and make strategic decisions with authority.

- **Communication:** Effective C-suite leaders communicate with clarity, conciseness, and conviction. They have the ability to articulate complex ideas in a way that is accessible and compelling to various stakeholders.

- **Appearance and Demeanor:** While executive presence is not solely about physical appearance, a well-groomed and professional look, combined with strong posture and body language, reinforces a leader's credibility.

- **Emotional Intelligence:** Understanding and managing one's emotions, as well as recognizing and influencing the emotions of others, is a crucial part of leading effectively.

- **Vision and Strategic Thinking:** Leaders with executive presence exhibit forward-thinking perspectives, inspiring confidence in their ability to steer the organization toward success.

- **Credibility and Authenticity:** Authenticity builds trust. Executives who align their words with their actions and demonstrate integrity earn respect from employees, board members, and investors alike.

## The Role of Executive Presence in the C-Suite

Executives in the C-suite set the tone for an entire organization. Their leadership style influences company culture, employee engagement, and the firm's overall reputation. Executive presence plays a pivotal role in the following areas:

- **Inspiring Confidence Among Stakeholders:** Investors, board members, and employees look to C-suite leaders for reassurance, particularly in uncertain times. Leaders who demonstrate composure and a clear strategic vision inspire trust and confidence.

- **Driving Organizational Change:** Change is inevitable in the business environment. Leaders with strong executive presence facilitate smooth transitions by effectively communicating the reasons behind changes and guiding teams through uncertainty. Confidence inspires stakeholders to buy in.

- **Enhancing Brand Reputation:** A CEO or C-suite

executive is often the face of the company. Their ability to speak with authority and credibility in public forums strengthens the company's reputation and market position.

- **Building and Retaining Top Talent:** Employees are more likely to be engaged and committed to a leader who exudes confidence, authenticity, and strategic clarity. Strong executive presence fosters a culture of accountability and motivation.

- **Navigating Crisis Situations:** Whether managing a PR crisis or an economic downturn, leaders with executive presence maintain composure, communicate effectively, and take decisive actions that stabilize the organization.

## Case Studies: CEOs with Strong Executive Presence

### ***Horacio Rozanski, Booz Allen Hamilton***

Booz Allen Hamilton, a mid-cap consulting firm specializing in technology and security solutions, has seen significant growth under the leadership of Horacio Rozanski, who became CEO in 2015. His executive presence has been evident in several ways:

- **Strategic Vision:** In his first 10 years as CEO, Rozanski led Booz Allen through a digital transformation, positioning the company as a leader in cybersecurity and AI-driven consulting services. His ability to articulate a forward-looking vision has been instrumental in securing government and private-sector contracts.

- **Confident Communication:** Whether addressing investors, employees, or policymakers, Rozanski speaks with clarity and conviction. His ability to simplify complex industry challenges into digestible insights reinforces his credibility.

- **Commitment to Diversity and Inclusion:** Rozanski's leadership emphasizes creating an inclusive corporate culture, demonstrating emotional intelligence and authenticity.

- **Crisis Management:** During periods of uncertainty, such as the COVID-19 pandemic, Rozanski maintained transparency and provided clear strategic direction to ensure business continuity.

***Aneel Bhusri, Workday***

Aneel Bhusri, co-founder and CEO of Workday, a leading provider of enterprise cloud applications for finance and human resources, exemplifies executive presence through:

- **Visionary Leadership:** Bhusri's ability to anticipate industry trends has kept Workday at the forefront of cloud-based enterprise solutions.

- **Authentic and Approachable Leadership:** Known for his down-to-earth demeanor, Bhusri strikes a balance between approachability and authority, making employees and stakeholders feel valued and engaged.

- **Effective Public Speaking:** Whether at industry conferences or investor meetings, he presents complex software and business strategies in a compelling and accessible manner.

- **Crisis Resilience:** In response to economic downturns, Bhusri demonstrated agility, making strategic decisions that ensured long-term growth while maintaining employee morale.

## Developing Executive Presence

Aspiring C-suite leaders and current executives looking to refine their executive presence can try these strategies:

- **Seek Feedback:** Understanding how others perceive you is essential. Soliciting feedback from mentors, peers, and executive coaches can provide insights into areas for improvement.

- **Practice Public Speaking:** Strong communication skills are developed over time. Taking advantage of speaking engagements, media training, and executive coaching can enhance articulation and persuasion skills.

- **Develop Emotional Intelligence:** Leaders should

cultivate self-awareness, empathy, and active listening skills to enhance their influence and decision-making capabilities.

- **Invest in Professional Development:** Attending leadership seminars, executive education programs, and networking events can provide valuable learning opportunities.
- **Maintain a Confident Presence:** Body language, tone of voice, and overall demeanor contribute significantly to executive presence. Practicing composure under pressure enhances credibility.

## Conclusion

Executive presence is a vital quality for C-suite leaders, particularly in small- and mid-cap companies where leadership can significantly impact growth, investor confidence, and corporate culture. Leaders like Horacio Rozanski and Aneel Bhusri exemplify how executive presence enhances business success through strategic vision, confident communication, and strong leadership.

For current and aspiring executives, developing executive presence involves projecting confidence, inspiring trust, demonstrating authenticity, and effectively leading organizations through both opportunities and challenges. By honing these skills, leaders can cultivate a compelling presence that drives sustained business success.

# Section III: Lead Under Pressure

## Your Calm Is Your Power

Resilience is one of the most critical attributes for executives operating in the C-suite of small and mid-sized companies. These leaders face immense pressure to drive growth, sustain profitability, manage crises, and navigate shifting market dynamics, all while maintaining stakeholder confidence and trust. The ability to adapt to adversity, make strategic pivots, and maintain a sharp vision under stress is what separates successful executives from those who falter.

## The Importance of Resilience in the C-Suite

Executives in the C-suite bear the responsibility of shaping the strategic direction of an organization while ensuring operational excellence. At any given time, the business landscape is unpredictable, characterized by economic fluctuations, technological disruptions, regulatory changes, and geopolitical instability. Smaller and mid-cap companies, which often operate with fewer resources than large corporations, are particularly vulnerable to such challenges.

Resilience in executive leadership manifests in several key areas:

- **Crisis Management:** The ability to navigate financial downturns, public relations crises, supply chain disruptions, and workforce challenges is critical. Resilient executives remain composed, decisive, and forward-thinking during turbulent times.

- **Adaptability and Innovation:** Companies must continuously evolve to remain competitive. Resilient leaders foster a culture of innovation, embrace change, and encourage their teams to experiment with new ideas.

- **Emotional Intelligence and Leadership Presence:** Strong leadership in the face of adversity requires high emotional intelligence. Executives must manage their own stress while providing reassurance and clarity to employees, investors, and customers.

- **Long-Term Vision with Short-Term Agility:** Resilient leaders balance immediate problem-solving with long-term strategic planning, ensuring their organizations remain viable and competitive.

## Attributes of Resilient Executives

Several characteristics define resilient C-suite leaders:

- **Decisiveness Under Pressure:** They make tough decisions quickly without succumbing to analysis paralysis.

- **Strong Communication Skills:** They articulate their vision clearly, inspiring confidence among their teams.

- **Empathy and Emotional Stability:** They remain connected with employees and stakeholders, providing guidance without being reactionary.

- **Continuous Learning and Growth Mindset:** They seek to learn from setbacks and improve their leadership approach.

- **Endurance and Perseverance:** They persist through challenges and stay optimistic, yet realistic.

## Case Studies: Resilient Executives in Mid-Cap Companies

### *Corey Barry, Best Buy*

Best Buy, historically known for its brick-and-mortar retail model, faced significant challenges with the rise of e-commerce giants like Amazon. Corey Barry, who assumed the CEO role in 2019, navigated the company through the digital transformation and the unexpected COVID-19 pandemic.

- **Resilience in Action**: Barry pivoted Best Buy's operations quickly, ramping up e-commerce capabilities, implementing curbside pickup models, and streamlining operations. Her ability to remain agile in crisis situations ensured the company's continued success.

- **Outcome**: Despite retail sector disruptions, Best Buy not only survived but expanded its market share, proving Barry's resilience as a leader.

***Brian Niccol, Chipotle Mexican Grill***

Chipotle faced significant challenges before Brian Niccol took over as CEO in 2018. The brand had suffered from food safety crises, negative press, and declining sales. Under Niccol's leadership, the company underwent a transformation that reinstated consumer trust and reinvigorated growth.

- **Resilience in Action**: Niccol focused on operational improvements, digital expansion, and marketing efforts to reposition Chipotle as a leader in fast-casual dining. He embraced technological advancements, including mobile ordering and delivery services, to modernize the company's customer experience.

- **Outcome**: Chipotle's stock and brand reputation saw a remarkable turnaround, solidifying Niccol as a strong example of an executive whose resilience successfully revived a struggling mid-cap brand.

## Conclusion

Resilience is a defining trait of successful C-suite executives, particularly in mid-cap companies where agility, innovation, and strategic foresight are vital for survival and growth. Executives like

Corey Barry and Brian Niccol exemplify how resilient leadership enables companies to navigate crises, adapt to market changes, and emerge stronger. As the business landscape continues to evolve, organizations must prioritize resilience in their executive teams to ensure long-term success and stability.

By fostering resilience, companies of any size can not only withstand adversity but also seize opportunities that lead to sustained growth and competitive advantage.

## Section IV: Stay Humble, Stay Strong

### Confidence Without Ego Wins

In the high-stakes world of corporate leadership, executives in the C-suite are often expected to be visionary, decisive, and confident. However, one often overlooked yet crucial characteristic of effective leaders is humility. Contrary to the outdated perception that humility signifies weakness, research and real-world examples show that humility fosters collaboration, innovation, and long-term success.

### Defining Humility in Leadership

Humility in leadership is characterized by self-awareness, openness to feedback, acknowledgment of mistakes, and a willingness to learn from others. It enables leaders to balance confidence with vulnerability, fostering a culture of trust and continuous improvement. For executives, humility does not mean a lack of ambition or authority; rather, it involves a measured understanding of one's strengths and weaknesses and an appreciation for the contributions of others.

## The Business Case for Humility in the C-Suite

Research suggests that humility in leadership is linked to improved employee engagement, ethical decision-making, and organizational performance. A 2018 study published in the *Journal of Management* found that companies led by humble CEOs tend to have stronger collaboration, higher-performing teams, and greater adaptability in the face of challenges (Ou et al, 2014). Some ways that humility benefits executives in the C-suite include:

- **Improved Decision-Making:** Humble leaders are more likely to seek diverse perspectives before making decisions. This mitigates the risks associated with overconfidence and groupthink, leading to more balanced and well-informed choices.

- **Enhanced Corporate Culture:** Employees are more likely to feel valued and empowered when their leaders demonstrate humility. By recognizing and celebrating the achievements of their teams, humble executives foster a culture of shared success, which improves morale and productivity.

- **Greater Adaptability and Resilience:** Humble executives acknowledge that they do not have all the answers and are open to learning from both successes and failures. This makes them more adaptable to changing market conditions and more resilient during crises.

## Case Studies: Humility in Large-Cap Companies

***Satya Nadella, Microsoft***

When Satya Nadella took over as CEO of Microsoft, the company was struggling with internal conflicts and a culture of competition rather than collaboration. One of Nadella's first priorities was to shift the corporate mindset from "know-it-all" to "learn-it-all." By fostering humility and a growth mindset, he encouraged innovation, promoted teamwork, and revitalized Microsoft's corporate culture.

Nadella's leadership style emphasized listening to employees, valuing customer feedback, and improving continuously. His humility-driven approach contributed to Microsoft's resurgence, with the company's market capitalization surpassing $2 trillion by 2021. His ability to admit mistakes, learn from competitors, and prioritize collective success cemented Microsoft's position as a global technology leader.

***Alan Mulally, Ford Motor Co.***

Another exemplary case of humility in the C-suite is Alan Mulally, who served as CEO of Ford from 2006 to 2014. When Mulally took over, Ford was facing financial difficulties and an impending bankruptcy. Rather than placing blame or making unilateral decisions, he approached the crisis with humility by listening to employees at all levels, openly addressing challenges, and fostering a culture of transparency.

Mulally implemented a "One Ford" strategy, emphasizing teamwork and collaboration over internal competition. He encouraged executives to admit when they face obstacles and to seek collective solutions rather than hiding problems. His leadership turned Ford around without requiring a government bailout, reinforcing the idea that humility can be a powerful driver of corporate success.

## Cultivating Humility in the C-Suite

For organizations seeking to instill humility in their leadership ranks, the following strategies can be effective:

- **Encourage Self-Reflection:** Providing leadership training and executive coaching can help senior leaders develop greater self-awareness.

- **Foster a Feedback-Rich Environment:** Creating channels for employees at all levels to provide honest feedback helps reinforce humility in leadership.

- **Recognize and Reward Humility:** Highlighting and celebrating humble leadership behaviors reinforces their value within the organization.

- **Model the Behavior:** When C-suite executives consistently demonstrate humility, they set a powerful precedent for the entire company.

## Conclusion

Humility in the C-suite is a catalyst for sustainable success. By fostering open communication, promoting collaboration, and demonstrating a willingness to learn, humble executives drive innovation, enhance employee engagement, and strengthen corporate resilience. As seen in the leadership of Satya Nadella at Microsoft and Alan Mulally at Ford, humility is a defining trait of transformative leaders who prioritize long-term growth over personal ego. Embracing humility is not just a moral imperative but a strategic advantage in the dynamic business landscape.

# 3

# Make People Want to Follow You

*People Follow Leaders Who Make Them Feel Seen, Heard, and Valued*

## Section I: Work Together

### Take Advantage of Expertise

Collaboration is a cornerstone of effective leadership in the C-suite. As companies grow and evolve, executives must work together to drive innovation, streamline decision-making, and ensure sustainable success. The days of siloed leadership are long gone. Today's business landscape demands a unified approach, where CFOs, CMOs, COOs, and other key leaders work in lockstep with the CEO to lead the organization effectively.

### Why Collaboration Is Essential

In the C-suite, every executive brings a different set of skills to the table. When any of those skill sets are missing, operations can't run at their most efficient level. Bringing them all together ensures the best outcome.

**Cross-functional decision making**

No single executive can oversee every aspect of a company's operations effectively. By fostering a culture of collaboration, C-suite leaders bring their unique expertise to the table, ensuring well-rounded decision-making. For example, a CFO's financial acumen complements the CMO's market insights, while a COO's operational focus aligns with the CTO's technological strategies. These interactions drive balanced, strategic growth.

**Innovation and agility**

Collaboration fosters innovation by encouraging diverse perspectives. A culture of open communication allows executives to challenge assumptions, identify new opportunities, and respond rapidly to market shifts. The best ideas often emerge when leaders with different areas of expertise work together to solve complex challenges.

**Organizational alignment**

A lack of collaboration can lead to misalignment, where different departments work toward different objectives. When the C-suite functions as a cohesive unit, strategic goals are clear and aligned throughout the organization. This unity enhances efficiency, improves employee morale, and ensures that all departments contribute to overarching business objectives.

**Effective crisis management**

During times of crisis such as economic downturns or industry disruptions, collaborative leadership is crucial. When executives work together, they can devise comprehensive solutions that consider financial, operational, technological, and human capital implications. A well-integrated C-suite ensures resilience and adaptability while navigating crises.

## CEOs Who Exemplify Collaborative Leadership

***Satya Nadella, Microsoft***

Microsoft's transformation from stagnation to industry leader began when CEO Satya Nadella began to focus on collaboration and teamwork. Nadella encouraged cross-functional cooperation, shifting the company's focus toward cloud computing and AI-driven solutions. By fostering a collaborative environment between product teams, engineering, and marketing, he scaled Microsoft's cloud business and re-established the company as a technology leader. His ability to bring together key executives—particularly CFO Amy Hood and CPO Kathleen Hogan—was instrumental in Microsoft's resurgence.

***Shantanu Narayen, Adobe***

Shantanu Narayen's leadership at Adobe displayed the power of collaboration in scaling a company. When he took over as

CEO in 2007, Adobe was heavily reliant on boxed software sales. Recognizing the need for change, Narayen collaborated closely with his executive team to transition Adobe to a cloud-based subscription model. This required seamless collaboration between the finance, technology, marketing, and sales teams. The shift to Adobe Creative Cloud was a monumental success, significantly increasing recurring revenue and ensuring long-term growth.

## Strategies to Foster Collaboration in the C-Suite

Siloed leadership has become a death knell for companies that want to sustain growth. Success depends on each executive's contributions.

**Establish clear communication channels.**

Open communication is the foundation of collaboration. C-suite executives must regularly engage in transparent discussions, whether through structured meetings or informal check-ins. Digital collaboration tools such as Slack, Microsoft Teams, and Zoom can facilitate ongoing dialogue.

**Encourage a culture of trust and respect.**

Trust is essential for effective collaboration. Executives should be encouraged to voice their opinions without fear of conflict. A culture where leaders respect each other's expertise and actively listen to different viewpoints fosters a more cohesive leadership team.

**Align goals and incentives.**

C-suite executives must be working toward the same strategic objectives for businesses to succeed. This is critical. Companies should determine how to align key performance indicators (KPIs) across departments to encourage joint accountability and shared success.

**Promote cross-departmental initiatives.**

Initiatives that require multiple departments to collaborate, such as product development or customer experience enhancements, should be prioritized. By assigning cross-functional leadership roles to executives, companies can reinforce the importance of teamwork.

**Invest in leadership development.**

Companies should provide training and coaching programs that emphasize collaboration skills. Executive retreats, leadership workshops, and peer mentoring can help strengthen teamwork at the highest levels of the organization. Companies that prioritize collaboration training and set clear expectations operate more creatively and efficiently.

## Conclusion

Companies looking to thrive in an increasingly complex and competitive business environment must foster collaboration within the C-suite. Executives who prioritize teamwork, communication, and cross-functional cooperation position their organizations for long-term success. By embracing a culture of unity at the executive level, businesses can drive innovation, enhance decision-making, and maintain agility in a rapidly changing world.

# **Section II: Inspire Action**

## Influence Comes From Intention, Not Volume

C-suite executives must possess a wide range of skills beyond technical expertise. Among these, coaching and mentorship stand out as critical capabilities that drive organizational growth, talent development, and sustainable success. Effective coaching and mentorship by senior executives not only enhance workforce performance but also shape future leaders, foster a strong company culture, and provide a competitive edge in the marketplace.

## The Role of Coaching in Executive Leadership

Coaching in the C-suite is a powerful tool for developing both individual and organizational capabilities. Coaching, unlike traditional management approaches, emphasizes empowerment, accountability, and self-improvement. It involves guiding employees and other executives through challenges, helping them build confidence, and supporting their professional growth. Executives who actively coach their teams create an environment where employees feel valued, engaged, and motivated to perform at their best.

## Benefits of Coaching in the C-Suite

- **Enhanced Leadership Development:** Senior leaders who coach their subordinates help cultivate the next generation of executives. By sharing their experiences and providing constructive feedback, they prepare high-potential employees for future leadership roles.

- **Improved Decision-Making:** Coaching encourages executives to reflect on their decision-making processes, which fosters critical thinking and strategic planning skills that drive business success.

- **Increased Employee Engagement:** A coaching culture fosters a sense of purpose and belonging among employees, resulting in higher retention rates and enhanced job satisfaction.

- **Stronger Organizational Resilience:** Leaders who embrace coaching create adaptable, forward-thinking teams capable of navigating change effectively.
- **Higher Performance Metrics:** Coaching-oriented leadership often sees better financial results because motivated employees drive productivity and innovation.

## The Impact of Mentorship in the C-Suite

Mentorship complements coaching by providing long-term career guidance and professional development. Unlike coaching, which focuses on immediate challenges and skill-building, mentorship is a sustained relationship centered on personal growth, sharing of wisdom and experience, and professional networking.

## Benefits of Mentorship in Executive Leadership

- **Knowledge Transfer:** Experienced executives passing down institutional knowledge ensure that core business principles and best practices endure across generations.
- **Diversity and Inclusion:** Mentorship programs help break barriers by supporting underrepresented employees in leadership pipelines.

- **Career Advancement:** Employees with strong mentors often rise to leadership roles faster due to direct exposure to leadership insights and opportunities.

- **Stronger Organizational Culture:** A mentorship-driven leadership approach builds trust, collaboration, and a culture of continuous learning.

- **Crisis Management and Adaptability:** Employees mentored by seasoned executives are better equipped to manage challenges, particularly in dynamic industries.

## Case Studies: Leading Through Coaching and Mentorship

***Hubert Joly, Best Buy***

Hubert Joly's approach to leadership as a former CEO at Best Buy provides invaluable insights for organizational leaders. As a former CEO, Joly transformed Best Buy by implementing a people-first leadership style that emphasized coaching and mentorship. He personally mentored store managers and executives, fostering a leadership pipeline that empowered employees at all levels. His "human magic" philosophy helped Best Buy rebound from financial struggles and establish a thriving culture of mentorship.

Here are some key takeaways from Joly's experience:

- Invest time in personally mentoring key employees.

- Develop a leadership philosophy centered on people rather than just profits.
- Encourage managers to function as coaches within their departments.

***Melissa Reiff, The Container Store***

Melissa Reiff, former CEO of the mid-cap retailer The Container Store, prioritized mentorship as a cornerstone of her leadership strategy. Under her tenure, she championed a company culture based on servant leadership, where executives actively mentored employees. Reiff's leadership model empowered employees, increased engagement, and led to consistent financial performance.

Some key strategies for mid-cap CEOs from Reiff's tenure at The Container Store include:

- Implement mentorship programs at all levels of the organization.
- Encourage senior leaders to engage in one-on-one development conversations with employees.
- Foster a workplace culture where coaching is a shared responsibility.

## Implementing Coaching and Mentorship

1. **Establish a Coaching Culture:** Encourage executives

to function as coaches rather than traditional top-down managers.

2. **Formalize Mentorship Programs:** Pair emerging leaders with seasoned executives to create structured mentorship relationships.

3. **Encourage Continuous Learning:** Provide leadership development programs that reinforce coaching methodologies.

4. **Leverage Technology:** Use digital tools to facilitate mentorship programs, track progress, and assess leadership development.

5. **Measure Success:** Implement KPIs to assess the impact of coaching and mentorship on employee retention, engagement, and productivity.

## Conclusion

Incorporating coaching and mentorship as core characteristics of the C-suite leads to sustainable business success. By fostering a culture of learning, guidance, and development, executives can build resilient organizations that thrive in competitive markets. CEOs like Hubert Joly and Melissa Reiff reinforce the idea that investing in people leads to stronger business outcomes. Companies that prioritize these leadership traits will not only drive growth but also cultivate a lasting legacy of innovation and empowerment.

# Section III: Lead Through Conflict

## Avoiding Friction Leads to Failure

Conflict is an inevitable aspect of business, particularly at the executive level where high-stakes decisions, competing interests, and intense personalities converge. For any size organization, conflict resolution policies are crucial for maintaining operational efficiency, fostering a healthy corporate culture, and driving sustained growth. The C-suite must actively implement and adhere to robust conflict resolution strategies to ensure that disputes are overseen effectively before they escalate into detrimental issues.

## The Need for Conflict Resolution in the C-Suite

### Protecting company performance and productivity

Unchecked conflicts at the executive level can slow decision-making, reduce productivity, and create an environment of mistrust. According to a study by CPP Global, unresolved workplace conflict costs U.S. businesses approximately $359 billion annually in lost productivity (*Workplace conflict and how*

..., 2008). For small- and mid-cap organizations, the financial and reputational risks associated with executive disputes can be particularly damaging.

## Enhancing leadership cohesion

The C-suite comprises highly skilled and ambitious leaders, each with distinct viewpoints and strategic priorities. Without a structured approach to resolving conflicts, executives may engage in counterproductive behaviors such as passive-aggressive styles, silo-building, or outright hostility. Establishing a formal conflict resolution framework ensures that differences are addressed constructively, reinforcing leadership unity.

## Safeguarding company culture

Employees look to the C-suite for behavioral cues. If executives model effective conflict resolution, they set the precedent for the rest of the organization, fostering a culture of transparency, respect, and collaboration. Conversely, visible discord among senior leaders can create anxiety, reduce employee engagement, and contribute to high turnover rates.

## Mitigating legal and reputational risks

Poorly handled conflicts can lead to legal disputes, regulatory scrutiny, and reputational damage. A 2021 PwC report on corporate governance emphasized that boards and shareholders are increasingly holding executives accountable for their interpersonal dynamics (*PwC 2021 Annual* ..., 2021). Having a clear conflict resolution protocol can minimize legal exposure and protect an organization's brand.

## Best Practices for Conflict Resolution in the C-Suite

**Establish clear policies and procedures.**

Companies should develop formal conflict resolution guidelines outlining:

- the steps for addressing executive disputes.
- the role of mediators, whether internal (HR professionals) or external (executive coaches).
- the escalation process for conflicts that cannot be resolved internally.

**Encourage open communication.**

Building a culture of psychological safety—where executives feel comfortable expressing concerns without fear of retaliation—is essential. Regular and structured executive meetings focused on alignment and issue resolution can help prevent conflicts from festering.

**Use mediation and third-party intervention.**

In cases where internal resolution efforts fail, bringing in professional mediators or executive coaches can provide impartial perspectives and facilitate productive discussions.

**Implement conflict resolution training.**

Even experienced executives can benefit from training in negotiation, emotional intelligence, and dispute resolution techniques. Programs such as those offered by Harvard's Program on Negotiation or the International Institute for Conflict Prevention and Resolution (CPR) provide valuable tools for C-suite leaders.

**Hold leaders accountable.**

Establishing metrics for executive collaboration and conflict management as part of annual performance reviews can reinforce the importance of these skills. Some organizations incorporate 360-degree feedback mechanisms to gather insights from peers, subordinates, and board members.

## Case Studies: Mid-Cap CEOs Leading Conflict Resolution

***Arne Sorenson, Marriott International***

Though Marriott International is a large enterprise, former CEO Arne Sorenson's approach to conflict resolution offers valuable lessons for small- and mid-cap companies. Sorenson, who led Marriott through significant acquisitions and industry disruptions, emphasized transparency and open dialogue as key conflict resolution tools. He championed an executive culture where disagreements were openly discussed and resolved through structured, mediated discussions. Mid-cap CEOs have since adopted his model, implementing clear communication strategies and mediation processes to prevent executive disputes from escalating.

***Scott Dorsey, ExactTarget***

Scott Dorsey, co-founder and former CEO of ExactTarget, who led the mid-cap digital marketing company before its acquisition by Salesforce, was known for fostering a collaborative executive team. He implemented structured conflict resolution training for senior leaders, ensuring that disagreements were addressed promptly and constructively. By promoting a leadership culture centered on mutual respect and problem-solving through initiative, Dorsey effectively scaled the company while minimizing internal friction.

## Conclusion

For small- and mid-cap organizations, strong conflict resolution policies in the C-suite make sustainable growth possible. By implementing clear protocols, fostering open communication, leveraging third-party mediation, and holding leaders accountable, companies can prevent conflicts from undermining their strategic objectives. Conflict resolution can be integrated into corporate governance, ultimately leading to more cohesive and resilient leadership teams.

As businesses navigate complex market dynamics, conflicts at the executive level are inevitable, and long-term success depends on prioritizing their resolution. By establishing clear protocols, organizations can protect their productivity, culture, and reputation while fostering a leadership team capable of driving innovation and sustained performance.

# Section IV: Grow Leaders, Not Followers

## Coaching Beats Control

Persuasiveness is a crucial trait for C-suite executives, as it significantly influences their ability to drive organizational success, secure stakeholder buy-in, and inspire teams toward a shared vision. In small- and mid-cap companies, where resource constraints and competitive pressures are particularly acute, an executive's ability to persuade can make the difference between stagnation and exponential growth.

## Why Persuasiveness Matters for C-Suite Executives

As leaders, executives in the C-suite rely on their ability to convince employees and other stakeholders to focus on the desired outcomes. Their skills affect their companies in many different ways.

### Influencing internal and external stakeholders

Executives must secure the commitment of various stakeholders, including employees, board members, investors, and customers. Persuasive communication fosters alignment between a company's strategic objectives and the interests of these groups. Without strong persuasive abilities, even the best ideas may fail due to a lack of buy-in.

### Driving organizational change

Change management is a critical component of leadership, particularly for businesses facing market volatility and evolving industry dynamics. Persuasive leaders craft compelling narratives that help employees understand and embrace change, whether it involves adopting modern technologies, restructuring operations, or shifting corporate strategy.

## Negotiating strategic deals

While securing investment, negotiating supplier contracts, and forming strategic partnerships, C-suite executives must excel in persuasion to achieve favorable outcomes. The ability to articulate value propositions and align interests ensures that deals contribute to long-term growth.

## Inspiring and motivating teams

Executives must rally their workforce around a compelling vision. Persuasiveness enables leaders to inspire confidence, instill purpose, and raise the levels of engagement and productivity in their employees. This is particularly crucial in smaller and mid-cap companies, where agility and team cohesion can make the difference between success and failure.

## Enhancing corporate reputation

A persuasive executive can elevate a company's public image by effectively communicating its strengths, values, and market differentiation. Whether engaging with the media, speaking at industry conferences, or managing crises, the ability to craft and deliver convincing messages strengthens the brand.

## Case Studies: Persuasive Mid-Cap Executives

***Ritch Allison, Domino's Pizza***

Ritch Allison demonstrated exceptional persuasive abilities during his tenure as CEO of Domino's Pizza, a mid-cap company that experienced significant growth under his leadership between 2018 and 2022. Facing a highly competitive industry and shifting consumer preferences, Allison successfully championed a digital transformation strategy that positioned Domino's as a technology-driven pizza brand.

- **Digital innovation:** When Allison proposed investing heavily in online ordering, AI-driven customer service, and a robust delivery infrastructure, some investors were initially skeptical. However, through compelling presentations and clear data-driven arguments, he secured buy-in, resulting in a market-leading digital experience that significantly boosted revenue.

- **Embracing change:** As the company expanded its digital capabilities, Allison effectively communicated the benefits to employees, ensuring smooth adoption and alignment across teams.

- **Building consumer trust:** His persuasive messaging reinforced the company's commitment to quality and convenience, strengthening customer loyalty and brand reputation.

***Marillyn Hewson, Lockheed Martin***

Although Lockheed Martin grew to become a large enterprise, much of its growth trajectory can be attributed to Marillyn Hewson's leadership as CEO when it was operating at a mid-cap scale within certain divisions. Hewson's persuasive abilities were instrumental in securing government contracts, driving innovation, and strengthening stakeholder confidence.

- **Negotiating government contracts:** Hewson was known for her ability to articulate the value of Lockheed Martin's aerospace and defense solutions to government agencies, which led to multi-billion-dollar deals that fueled the company's expansion.

- **Leading cultural transformation:** She persuaded internal teams to embrace a culture of innovation and operational efficiency, driving significant improvements in product development and customer satisfaction.

- **Investor relations and public perception:** Hewson's persuasive leadership reassured investors during economic downturns, emphasizing the company's resilience and long-term strategic vision.

## Developing Persuasive Leadership Skills

Executives looking to strengthen their persuasive abilities can benefit from adopting the following strategies:

- **Master storytelling:** Effective persuasion often hinges on storytelling. Executives should craft narratives that evoke emotion, highlight real-world impact, and reinforce the company's mission.

- **Use data to drive communication:** Combining qualitative and quantitative insights enhances credibility, which builds trust with the audience. Leaders must present compelling data to support their arguments and sway skeptical stakeholders.

- **Listen actively and with empathy:** Persuasion is not just about speaking; it also involves understanding the concerns and motivations of others. Executives who actively listen and demonstrate empathy build trust and increase their influence.

- **Maintain personal credibility and authenticity:** A leader's persuasiveness is directly tied to their credibility. Executives must align their words with actions, consistently demonstrating integrity and expertise.

- **Practice public speaking and negotiation:** Regular practice in public speaking, media engagement, and high-stakes negotiations builds skills and enhances an executive's comfort level with communicating persuasively in different scenarios.

## Conclusion

Persuasiveness is a defining trait of successful C-suite executives, particularly in small- and mid-cap companies where resourcefulness and influence are paramount. Leaders like Ritch Allison and Marillyn Hewson exemplify how persuasive communication drives innovation, secures stakeholder buy-in, and fuels business growth. By mastering storytelling, leveraging data, practicing active listening, and honing negotiation skills, executives can enhance their persuasive abilities and drive sustained success.

# 4

# Lead the Change, Don't Chase It

*Stay Agile, Bet Smart, Lead Fearlessly*

## Section I: Adapt Like a Pro

### Be Fast, Not Frantic

Agility—the ability to pivot, adapt to market shifts, and make data-driven decisions at speed—is a critical competency for C-suite executives. Organizations that lack agility risk falling behind their competitors, losing market relevance, or becoming obsolete.

### The Importance of Agility in the C-Suite

#### Navigating market disruptions

The modern business environment is marked by continuous disruption driven by technological advancements, geopolitical shifts, regulatory changes, and economic uncertainties. Agile leaders have the ability to assess these disruptions and swiftly adjust their strategies to mitigate risks and capture new opportunities. The COVID-19 pandemic, for instance, underscored the need for adaptability as organizations had to transition to remote work, digital operations, and new business models overnight.

## Encouraging innovation and adaptability

C-suite leaders must develop a culture of continuous innovation, enabling their organizations to stay ahead of industry trends. By fostering agility, executives create an environment where employees are encouraged to experiment, iterate, and embrace change. Agile companies often leverage cross-functional teams, rapid prototyping, and real-time data to drive innovation at scale.

## Enhancing decision-making processes

Traditional decision-making processes, characterized by hierarchical approvals and lengthy deliberations, no longer serve the needs of fast-moving industries. Agility in leadership involves empowering teams with decentralized decision-making capabilities. Agile C-suite executives leverage real-time data analytics, scenario planning, and agile methodologies to make informed and timely decisions.

### Customer-centricity and market responsiveness

An agile C-suite ensures that customer needs remain at the core of business decisions. Organizations that respond swiftly to changing consumer preferences, emerging market trends, and feedback loops outperform those that are rigid in their approach. This customer-centric agility allows for personalized experiences, enhanced engagement, and sustained loyalty.

## Key Drivers of Agility in Leadership

### Flexible organizational structures

Traditional, hierarchical structures can impede agility. Many agile companies adopt networked or flat structures, reducing bureaucratic layers and enhancing communication and collaboration across departments. This structural flexibility allows leadership teams to react more quickly to external changes.

### Data-driven decision making

Agile leaders embrace digital transformation, leveraging real-time analytics, artificial intelligence, and machine learning to make informed strategic decisions. Data-driven insights enable initiative-taking adjustments in operations, marketing, finance, and customer service, ensuring competitiveness in dynamic markets.

### Empowered and cross-functional teams

Agility is not solely a top-down initiative; it requires buy-in from the entire organization. By fostering a culture where employees are empowered to experiment, make decisions, and collaborate across functions, C-suite executives enhance organizational resilience and adaptability.

### Resilient leadership mindset

Agile leaders embrace uncertainty, viewing challenges as opportunities rather than threats. They prioritize continuous learning, adaptability, and resilience, ensuring their organizations remain robust in the face of disruption.

## Case Studies: Agile Leaders in Small- and Mid-Cap Companies

### ***Frank Slootman, Snowflake***

Frank Slootman, CEO of Snowflake, demonstrated agility in leadership by spearheading the rapid growth of the company's cloud data platform. Under his leadership, Snowflake transitioned from a niche data storage provider to a dominant force in the cloud computing space. Slootman's ability to adapt Snowflake's product offerings in response to evolving customer needs and market dynamics exemplifies agile leadership. His focus on speed, execution, and continuous iteration enabled Snowflake to sustain a competitive edge in a highly dynamic industry.

***Aneel Bhusri, Workday***

As co-CEO of Workday, Aneel Bhusri successfully led the company through various phases of growth by embracing agility in innovation and customer engagement. By integrating artificial intelligence and machine learning into Workday's HR and fiscal management software, Bhusri ensured the company would remain at the forefront of enterprise software solutions. His ability to pivot Workday's strategy in response to technological shifts and customer feedback highlighted the significance of agility in executive leadership.

## Conclusion

Agility in the C-suite is a prerequisite for sustained success in today's fast-paced business environment. From navigating market disruptions to fostering innovation, enhancing decision-making, and maintaining customer-centricity, agile leadership is a defining factor for high-performing organizations. Leaders like Frank Slootman and Aneel Bhusri exemplify how agility enables companies to adapt, innovate, and thrive amid uncertainty. As organizations continue to face new challenges and opportunities, the ability of the C-suite to lead with agility will determine long-term resilience and growth.

# Section II: Bet Boldly, Not Blindly

## Risk Is the Price of Relevance

For companies looking to scale, risk is unavoidable. Scaling requires a delicate balance between seizing opportunities and managing potential pitfalls. Central to this process is the willingness to embrace risk factors that can propel a company toward significant growth when navigated effectively. The C-suite, particularly the CEO, plays a pivotal role in guiding these organizations through this landscape, making strategic decisions that involve calculated risks to achieve sustainable expansion.

## The Imperative of Risk-Taking in Scaling

Risk-taking is integral to business growth. It involves making decisions that, while uncertain, have the potential to yield substantial rewards. This might mean entering new markets, investing in innovative technologies, or redefining business models. Such actions can differentiate a company from its competitors and open avenues for increased revenue and market share.

However, risk-taking must be measured and strategic. Reckless decisions can lead to financial losses and reputational damage. Therefore, it is essential for leadership to assess risks thoroughly, weighing potential benefits against possible drawbacks. This strategic approach to risk ensures that the company is not only prepared to capitalize on opportunities but also resilient enough to overcome challenges that may arise.

## The Role of the C-Suite in Risk Management

The C-suite sets the strategic direction of the company. In the context of scaling, this leadership team must foster a culture that encourages innovation and calculated risk-taking. This involves:

- **Establishing a Risk Management Framework:** Developing comprehensive policies and procedures that identify potential risks, assess their impact, and outline mitigation strategies. This framework serves as a road map for decision-making, ensuring that all risks are considered and managed appropriately.

- **Integrating Risk into Strategic Planning:** Risk management should be a core component of the company's strategic plan. This integration ensures that as the company pursues growth opportunities, it remains cognizant of the associated risks and is prepared to address them.

- **Promoting a Risk-Aware Culture:** Encouraging open communication about risks at all organizational levels fosters an environment where employees feel empowered to identify and report potential issues. This culture of transparency enables the company to proactively manage risks before they escalate.

- **Leveraging Technology and Data:** Using advanced analytics and technology can enhance a company's ability to identify and assess risks. Data-driven insights provide a more accurate understanding of potential challenges and inform better decision-making.

## Case Studies: Successful Risk-Taking by Mid-Cap CEOs

***Aubrey McClendon, Chesapeake Energy***

Aubrey McClendon, co-founder and former CEO of Chesapeake Energy, exemplified strategic risk-taking in the energy sector. In 1989, at the age of 29, McClendon co-founded Chesapeake Energy, which was focused on drilling wells into unconventional reservoirs such as fractured carbonates and shales. He was an early adopter of horizontal drilling and hydraulic fracturing techniques, which were innovative and carried significant risk at the time. This approach led to rapid growth, and by 1993, the company became public. From 1994 to 1997, Chesapeake's stock was the most successful in the country, rising 274% in value. McClendon's willingness to embrace innovative technologies and methodologies transformed Chesapeake into a major player in the energy industry.

***Peter Zaffino, Marsh & McLennan Companies***

During his tenure as CEO of Guy Carpenter and later as CEO of Marsh, both subsidiaries of Marsh & McLennan

Agency, Peter Zaffino demonstrated effective risk management and strategic growth in the insurance and benefits industry. At Guy Carpenter, he streamlined operations, improved profitability, and made strategic acquisitions. Later, as CEO of Marsh, he led the company through significant growth, including the expansion of Marsh & McLennan Agency. Zaffino's strategic decisions involved calculated risks that contributed to the scaling and diversification of services within the company.

## Guidance for Effective Risk-Taking

Risk-taking is essential for growing a business because it drives innovation, opens new opportunities, and enables companies to stay ahead of competitors. For companies aiming to scale, the following strategies can facilitate effective risk-taking:

- **Develop a Comprehensive Risk Management Strategy:** Establish clear processes for identifying, assessing, and mitigating risks. This strategy should align with the company's overall objectives and be integrated into daily operations.

- **Foster a Culture of Innovation:** Encourage employees to think creatively and propose the latest ideas. A culture that rewards innovation will naturally embrace calculated risks.

- **Ensure Leadership Alignment:** The C-suite must present a united front regarding risk appetite and management. Consistent messaging from leadership reinforces the importance of strategic risk-taking.

- **Invest in Data and Analytics:** Leveraging data can provide insights into potential risks and opportunities, enabling more informed decision-making.
- **Learn from Failures:** Not all risks will result in success. It is crucial to analyze failures, extract lessons from them, and apply those lessons to future endeavors.

## Conclusion

Risk-taking is a fundamental component of scaling a company. When approached strategically, it can lead to significant growth and competitive advantage. The C-suite's role in fostering a risk-aware culture, developing robust risk-management frameworks, and leading by example is critical. By studying successful mid-cap CEOs, companies can gain valuable insights into balancing risk and reward during their growth journeys.

# Section III: Lead Through the Storm

## Real Leadership Shows Up in Crisis

Crisis management is one of the most critical responsibilities of the C-suite, particularly for CEOs, CFOs, and other senior executives. The ability to navigate crises effectively can determine the survival and success of a company. The C-suite's role in crisis management extends beyond merely responding to problems—it requires strategic foresight, disciplined execution, and resilience to steer the organization toward stability and growth.

## The Role of the C-Suite in Crisis Management

### Initiative-taking preparedness and risk assessment

The most effective crisis management strategies begin with initiative-taking preparedness. C-suite executives must implement risk assessment frameworks to identify potential threats before they escalate. This includes financial risks, cybersecurity threats, supply chain disruptions, reputational damage, and regulatory changes.

C-suite leaders must work closely with risk management teams to develop contingency plans, conduct stress tests, and establish clear protocols for crisis response. Scenario planning and crisis simulations can help executives and employees react swiftly and effectively when challenges arise.

### Decisive leadership and clear communication

A crisis can quickly erode trust among stakeholders, employees, and customers. The C-suite must demonstrate decisive leadership by making informed decisions promptly. Effective crisis communication is equally vital. CEOs and senior executives should maintain transparency, acknowledge issues, and provide clear guidance on the company's next steps.

During crises, stakeholders look to leadership for stability. C-suite executives must maintain a consistent message, using multiple communication channels to ensure that employees, investors, and customers remain well-informed. An empathetic approach helps preserve morale and trust, ultimately aiding in the company's recovery.

## Financial resilience and strategic decision-making

Financial stability is a crucial component of crisis management. CFOs and other financial leaders must ensure that the company has sufficient liquidity, diversified revenue streams, and cost-cutting strategies to weather economic downturns. A well-structured financial plan allows businesses to navigate prolonged periods of uncertainty without compromising operations or long-term growth.

Strategic decision-making in times of crisis often involves making difficult choices, such as restructuring, divestitures, or cost reductions. The C-suite must balance short-term survival with long-term sustainability, ensuring that crisis-driven decisions align with the company's overall vision and values.

## Case Studies: Successful Crisis Management by CEOs

### ***Howard Schultz, Starbucks' Post-2008 Revival***

Former Starbucks CEO Howard Schultz provided a master class in crisis management during the 2008 financial downturn. As consumer spending dropped and Starbucks faced declining sales, he implemented a strategic turnaround plan that included:

- closing underperforming stores to optimize operations.
- refocusing on core values, including customer experience and product quality.
- enhancing digital engagement and launching Starbucks Rewards to retain customers.
- investing in employee training and leadership development to improve service quality.

Schultz's ability to navigate the crisis through decisive leadership, financial discipline, and brand reinvigoration allowed Starbucks to emerge stronger, setting the foundation for sustained growth in the following decade.

### ***Mary Barra, Leading GM Through the Ignition Switch Crisis***

Mary Barra faced one of the most challenging corporate crises in recent history—the General Motors ignition switch recall scandal that occurred in 2014, less than a month after she had become the first female to be named CEO of one of the Big Three automakers.

When news was made public that faulty ignition switches had caused numerous accidents and fatalities, GM's reputation and financial stability were at stake. All eyes were on Barra.

Barra's crisis management strategy involved:

- taking full accountability and addressing the issue transparently.
- cooperating with regulators and ensuring swift action to address safety concerns.
- implementing a cultural transformation within GM to prioritize safety and ethical decision-making.
- strengthening quality control measures to prevent future issues.

Her initiative-taking and ethical leadership helped restore trust in GM, strengthening the company's position in the automotive industry.

## Lessons for the C-Suite

**Embrace transparency and accountability.**

Crisis situations demand honesty and responsibility. Attempting to conceal issues can lead to reputational damage and regulatory consequences. Companies that address problems openly tend to recover more effectively.

**Adaptability and agility are key.**

Rigid organizations struggle to manage crises effectively. The C-suite must foster a culture of adaptability, encouraging innovation and flexibility in response to challenges.

**Empower and support employees.**

Employees play a crucial role in crisis response. Providing them with the necessary resources, training, and support enables them to contribute effectively to the company's recovery efforts.

**Long-term vision over short-term fixes.**

While quick solutions may seem necessary, crisis management should align with the company's long-term goals. CEOs must resist the temptation to implement short-term fixes that could compromise future stability.

## Conclusion

Crisis management is an essential competency for the C-suite, as it demonstrates the company's resilience and sustainability. Executives who prepare proactively, communicate effectively, and make strategic financial decisions can navigate challenges while strengthening their organization's foundation. As demonstrated by Howard Schultz and Mary Barra, strong leadership in times of crisis not only mitigates risks but also positions companies for long-term success. The ability to manage crises with discipline and foresight is what separates exceptional leaders from the rest, making this skill a cornerstone of effective executive leadership.

## Section IV: Stay in Student Mode

### Curiosity Keeps You in the Game

In an era where industries evolve at an unprecedented pace, organizations must prioritize continuous learning to remain competitive. A company's ability to adapt, innovate, and scale depends on its workforce's capacity to acquire new skills and knowledge. This commitment to learning must be championed from the top, with the C-suite playing a crucial role in fostering an environment that encourages education, skill development, and intellectual curiosity.

### The Business Case for Continuous Learning

Modern organizations face numerous challenges, including technological advancements, shifting consumer behaviors, and increasing competition. To navigate these complexities, businesses must cultivate a learning-centric culture that enhances employee performance, fosters innovation, and drives long-term growth.

- **Enhancing Employee Capabilities:** A workforce equipped with up-to-date knowledge and skills is better positioned to execute business strategies effectively. Continuous learning enables employees to stay ahead of industry trends, master emerging technologies, and refine their expertise.

- **Fostering Innovation:** Organizations that encourage continuous learning tend to be more innovative. Employees who are exposed to innovative ideas and perspectives are more likely to develop creative solutions to business problems.

- **Improving Employee Retention and Engagement:** A strong learning culture signals that an organization values professional growth, leading to increased job satisfaction and lower turnover rates.

- **Adapting to Market Changes:** The business landscape is dynamic, requiring organizations to change strategies quickly. A culture of learning ensures that employees can adapt to changes and drive organizational success.

## How the C-Suite Can Support Constant Learning

The leadership team, particularly the CEO and C-suite executives, must actively promote and invest in learning initiatives to create a sustainable culture of development. Here are several strategies the C-suite can adopt:

**1. Lead by example.**

Executives who prioritize their own learning set a powerful precedent for the rest of the organization. When C-suite members actively engage in professional development, whether through industry conferences, executive coaching, or continuing education programs, they reinforce the importance of lifelong learning.

**2. Embed learning into corporate strategy.**

Learning should not be an afterthought but an integral part of the business strategy. The C-suite should collaborate with HR and department heads to align learning initiatives with business goals, ensuring that training programs address specific organizational needs.

**3. Allocate resources for learning and development.**

Investment in learning and development is critical for maintaining a knowledgeable workforce. The C-suite should ensure adequate budgets for training programs, online courses, workshops, and mentorship programs.

**4. Foster a culture of psychological safety.**

Employees must feel comfortable experimenting, failing, and learning from their mistakes. The C-suite can cultivate an environment where employees are encouraged to take risks, share insights, and grow without fear of repercussions.

**5. Encourage cross-departmental learning.**

Knowledge-sharing across departments fosters innovation and a deeper understanding of the organization's operations. Executives can establish mentorship programs, cross-functional teams, and collaborative learning opportunities to facilitate the exchange of knowledge.

**6. Leverage technology for learning.**

Digital learning platforms, AI-driven training modules, and microlearning tools can make education more accessible and engaging. The C-suite should champion the adoption of technology that enables employees to learn at their own pace while ensuring the content remains relevant and impactful.

**7. Recognize and reward learning initiatives.**

Acknowledging employees who invest in their learning journey can reinforce a culture of continuous improvement. Incentives such as tuition reimbursement, promotions tied to skill development, and public recognition for learning achievements can motivate employees to prioritize growth.

**8. Establish external learning partnerships.**

Collaborating with universities, professional associations, and industry experts can provide employees with access to world-class education. The C-suite should explore partnerships that bring valuable learning opportunities to the organization.

## Case Studies: CEO Champions of Lifelong Learning

***Satya Nadella, Microsoft***

Under Satya Nadella's leadership, Microsoft underwent a significant cultural transformation centered around a growth mindset. Nadella encouraged employees to adopt a learning-oriented approach, famously shifting the company's ethos from "know-it-all" to "learn-it-all." His emphasis on continuous learning played a pivotal role in Microsoft's resurgence as a technology leader.

***Elon Musk, Tesla, SpaceX, Neuralink***

Elon Musk exemplifies self-directed learning, frequently acquiring knowledge across multiple disciplines including aerospace engineering, artificial intelligence, and energy solutions without formal degrees in these fields. His commitment to learning permeates his companies, where he encourages engineers and employees to expand their skill sets continuously to solve complex problems.

## Conclusion

Constant learning is a requirement for organizations striving for growth and innovation. The C-suite must take an active role in fostering a culture of continuous education. Executives should focus on leading by example, allocating resources, leveraging technology, and rewarding learning initiatives. By championing lifelong learning, executives not only enhance their organization's competitive edge but also empower employees to reach their full potential, ensuring sustainable success in a rapidly evolving business landscape.

# 5

# Deliver What Moves the Needle

*Focus, Discipline, and Customer Obsession Separate Good Leaders from Great Ones*

## Section I: Focus Relentlessly

### Don't Confuse Busy With Productive

Accountability in the C-suite is another critical component of sustainable business success. Leaders at the highest level of an organization set the tone for company culture, financial performance, ethical standards, and strategic direction. Without strong accountability mechanisms, businesses risk inefficiency, ethical lapses, financial mismanagement, and reputational damage.

## Defining Accountability in the C-Suite

Accountability refers to the obligation of C-suite executives to take responsibility for their actions, decisions, and leadership effectiveness. It encompasses:

- **Financial Accountability:** Ensuring transparency in budgeting, financial reporting, and profitability.
- **Operational Accountability:** Executing strategic initiatives effectively and efficiently.
- **Ethical Accountability:** Upholding corporate social responsibility and ethical behavior.
- **Cultural Accountability:** Fostering a work environment based on integrity, inclusivity, and performance.

## The Risks of Poor Accountability

Lack of accountability in the C-suite can have disastrous consequences for businesses, including:

- **Erosion of Trust:** Employees, stakeholders, and customers lose confidence in leadership when executives fail to take responsibility for mistakes.

- **Legal and Regulatory Issues:** Poor accountability often leads to compliance violations, lawsuits, and regulatory penalties.

- **Financial Losses:** Mismanagement of company resources or fraudulent activities can lead to financial collapse.

- **Toxic Workplace Culture:** Employees may disengage, productivity can decline, and retention issues may arise when leadership lacks integrity.

Historical examples, such as the collapse of Enron and the 2008 financial crisis, illustrate the devastating effects of C-suite leaders failing to uphold accountability.

## Case Studies: How Top CEOs Build Accountability

### ***Satya Nadella, Microsoft***

Satya Nadella's transformation of Microsoft's culture included embedding accountability into leadership at all levels. His changes involved several aspects of the company's value system:

- **Growth Mindset and Cultural Shift:** Nadella emphasized a growth mindset, where leaders were expected to take responsibility for their personal development and company performance.

- **Clear Performance Metrics:** He introduced new performance evaluation models that focused on collaboration and impact rather than individual competition.

- **Transparency and Communication:** Nadella prioritized transparency in decision-making, regularly sharing Microsoft's strategic goals and challenges with employees and stakeholders.

- **Ethical Leadership:** Under his leadership, Microsoft invested heavily in AI ethics, cybersecurity, and corporate social responsibility, ensuring that executives remain accountable for the broader impact of technology.

***Ed Bastian, Delta Air Lines***

As CEO of Delta Air Lines, Ed Bastian fostered a culture of accountability that helped Delta maintain its reputation for strong customer service and operational excellence.

- **Customer-Centric Accountability:** Bastian ensured that customer satisfaction remained at the core of decision-making. He personally addressed customer concerns and encouraged employees to fly the airline so they understood the passenger experience.

- **Financial Responsibility:** Delta remained profitable even through turbulent times by maintaining disciplined financial planning and executive accountability.

- **Employee Engagement:** Bastian holds himself and his leadership team accountable for employee well-being, offering profit-sharing programs and career development opportunities.

- **Crisis Management:** During the COVID-19 pandemic, Bastian took steps to maintain financial stability, protect jobs, and keep the public informed, demonstrating transparency and responsibility.

## Implementing Accountability in the C-Suite

To ensure accountability, organizations should adopt the following best practices:

1. **Establish Clear Expectations:** Define key performance indicators (KPIs) and strategic goals that align with corporate values.

2. **Foster a Culture of Responsibility:** Encourage open communication, where employees at all levels feel empowered to hold leadership accountable.

3. **Implement Governance and Oversight Mechanisms:** Boards of directors must actively oversee executive performance and enforce accountability measures.

4. **Ensure Ethical Leadership:** C-suite executives should lead by example, demonstrating integrity and transparency in their decision-making.

5. **Review Performance Regularly:** Conducting frequent executive performance evaluations ensures that leaders are meeting their responsibilities effectively.

## Conclusion

Accountability in the C-suite is about maintaining corporate governance and is the foundation of sustainable success. Leaders like Satya Nadella and Ed Bastian exemplify how accountability-driven leadership fosters innovation, trust, and long-term growth. Companies that prioritize executive accountability will not only avoid financial and ethical pitfalls but will also build resilient and high-performing organizations.

# Section II: Run a Tight Ship

## Systems Scale What Hustle Can't

Along with accountability, business acumen is one of the most critical competencies for executives in the C-suite. It encompasses financial literacy, strategic decision-making, operational efficiency, and market awareness. Business leaders with strong business acumen can analyze financial statements, assess risk, optimize revenue, and make data-driven decisions that lead to growth and profitability.

C-suite executives must possess a deep understanding of how their decisions impact the company's financial health. The ability to read financial reports, evaluate investments, and manage cash flow is not just the responsibility of the CFO. The CEO, COO, and other senior executives must share that accountability. Without strong business acumen, a company is at risk of poor financial performance, inefficient operations, and missed opportunities.

## The Importance of Business Acumen in the C-Suite

### Strategic financial decision-making

Executives with business acumen can evaluate market trends, financial data, and industry dynamics to make strategic decisions. They understand how to allocate resources effectively and prioritize initiatives that drive long-term success. Without this skill, leaders may make costly mistakes that can damage a company's financial stability.

For example, an executive might be presented with an opportunity to acquire another company. Without financial literacy and strategic insight, they may overlook hidden risks such as debt, poor cash flow, or declining revenues in the acquired company. A well-rounded executive will conduct thorough due diligence, assessing whether the acquisition aligns with long-term business goals.

## Understanding key financial metrics

C-suite executives must understand key financial metrics such as revenue growth, gross margin, EBITDA (Earnings Before Interest, Taxes, Depreciation, and Amortization), return on investment (ROI), and cash flow. These metrics provide insights into a company's financial health and its ability to sustain growth.

- Revenue growth indicates whether the company is increasing its sales and market share.
- Gross margin measures how efficiently the company produces and sells its products or services.
- EBITDA provides a clearer picture of profitability by excluding nonoperational expenses.
- Return on investment helps assess whether an investment is generating value for the company.
- Cash flow ensures that a company has enough liquidity to operate effectively.

Executives who can accurately interpret these metrics can make informed decisions about pricing, cost-cutting, and capital allocation, resulting in better financial outcomes.

### Risk management and financial discipline

Every business faces financial risks, including market fluctuations, economic downturns, and regulatory changes. A C-suite executive with strong business acumen can anticipate risks and put contingency plans in place.

For instance, a CEO might try to diversify revenue streams by expanding into new markets. Without assessing financial risks like currency fluctuations, regulatory barriers, or high operating costs, this decision could backfire. Business acumen enables executives to balance risk and reward, ensuring sustainable growth.

Additionally, financial discipline is crucial in managing company budgets, reducing unnecessary expenses, and optimizing resources. Companies that lack financial discipline often struggle with high debt, cash flow problems, and poor profitability.

### Capital allocation and investment strategy

Allocating capital efficiently is a key role for the C-suite. Executives need to determine where to invest for the highest returns. This includes decisions on research and development, marketing, technology upgrades, and workforce expansion.

A well-informed CEO will allocate resources toward high-growth opportunities rather than overspending on unproven initiatives. For example, if a company operates in the tech industry, investing in artificial intelligence or cloud computing might yield higher returns than traditional IT infrastructure.

Additionally, executives must ensure that the company maintains a healthy balance sheet, avoiding excessive debt while maximizing shareholder value.

### Operational efficiency and cost management

Profitability means increasing revenue and controlling costs. Business acumen helps executives identify inefficiencies and implement cost-saving measures without compromising product quality or customer service.

One example of cost management is streamlining supply chains. A CEO with strong financial insight might renegotiate vendor contracts, adopt just-in-time inventory management, or invest in automation to reduce production costs.

By improving operational efficiency, companies can increase their margins and reinvest savings into growth initiatives.

### Financial communication and stakeholder management

A C-suite executive must communicate financial performance and strategy effectively to stakeholders, including investors, board members, and employees.

- Investors expect transparency in financial health and future growth prospects.

- Board members require data-driven insights to make governance decisions.

- Employees need to understand how financial decisions impact job security and company direction.

Executives who can articulate financial strategies in simple terms build trust and alignment across all levels of the organization.

## Key Financial Skills for C-Suite Executives

C-suite executives should master the following financial skills:

- **Financial Statement Analysis:** Understanding balance sheets, income statements, and cash flow statements.
- **Budgeting and Forecasting:** Planning and predicting financial outcomes.
- **Cost Control and Efficiency Optimization:** Reducing waste and improving profitability.
- **Investment Analysis and Capital Allocation:** Assessing where to invest company resources.
- **Risk Assessment and Mitigation:** Identifying financial vulnerabilities.
- **Valuation Techniques:** Determining company worth in mergers, acquisitions, or funding rounds.
- **Debt and Equity Financing:** Managing fundraising and capital structure.

## Case Studies: Mid-Cap CEOs with Strong Business Acumen

***Brian Niccol, Chipotle Mexican Grill***

Former CEO Brian Niccol became head of Chipotle in 2018, when the company was facing food safety scandals and declining revenue. With strong business acumen, he focused on financial turnaround strategies:

- **Revenue Growth:** Niccol invested in digital ordering and delivery services, leading to significant sales increases.
- **Operational Efficiency:** He streamlined kitchen processes, improving service speed and reducing costs.
- **Capital Allocation:** He allocated resources toward strategic marketing and customer engagement, rebuilding the brand's reputation.

Under Niccol's leadership, Chipotle's stock price skyrocketed, demonstrating the power of financial acumen in revitalizing a company.

***Mary Dillon, Ulta Beauty***

Mary Dillon was CEO of Ulta Beauty from 2013 to 2021, transforming the business into a market leader in retail cosmetics. Her financial strategies included:

- **Expansion:** Dillon invested in store openings and e-commerce, significantly increasing Ulta's market share.

- **Cost Management:** She optimized inventory and supply chains, improving profit margins.
- **Innovation Investment:** She directed capital toward customer loyalty programs and technology upgrades.

Dillon's financial leadership helped Ulta outperform competitors and achieve sustained revenue growth.

## Conclusion

Business acumen is essential for the C-suite, as financial decisions impact every aspect of a company's success. Executives must develop skills in financial analysis, budgeting, risk management, and capital allocation to drive growth and profitability. CEOs like Brian Niccol and Mary Dillon demonstrate how financial expertise can transform mid-cap companies, leading to strong shareholder returns and long-term stability.

# Section III: Obsess Over the Customer

## Their Truth Is Your Strategy

Companies that prioritize customer-centric thinking in their strategies tend to outperform their peers. Organizations that integrate customer needs into their decision-making processes, particularly at the C-suite level, create stronger brand loyalty, increase revenue, and drive sustainable growth. Well-managed companies leverage customer-centricity as a business strategy, with executive leadership taking a profound role in shaping the customer-first culture.

## Defining Customer-Centric Thinking

Customer-centric thinking puts the customer at the core of business decisions, ensuring that products, services, and interactions align with customer needs and expectations. Unlike traditional business models that prioritize operational efficiency or financial metrics, a customer-centric approach integrates customer feedback, behavioral data, and personalized experiences into business strategy. Key elements of this thinking include:

- **Understanding Customer Needs:** Using data analytics and direct customer engagement to identify pain points and expectations.

- **Creating Value-Driven Experiences:** Designing products and services that address customer challenges and add meaningful value.

- **Long-Term Customer Relationships:** Prioritizing lifetime customer value over short-term transactions.

- **C-Suite Leadership Commitment:** Ensuring top executives champion and model customer-centric behaviors.

- **Organizational Alignment:** Embedding customer-first values across all departments, from marketing to operations.

## The Role of the C-Suite in Customer-Centric Strategies

For a company to be truly customer-centric, its executive leadership must drive the initiative. C-suite leaders, including the CEO, CMO, and Chief Customer Officer (CCO), play a pivotal role in shaping an organization's culture, strategies, and policies. Below are some key ways the C-suite fosters customer-centricity:

### CEO's role: setting vision

The CEO is responsible for embedding customer-centricity into the company's mission and vision. This involves:

- advocating for a culture that prioritizes customer satisfaction.
- ensuring investments in technology and resources that enhance customer experience.
- aligning corporate goals with customer-driven outcomes.

**CMO's role: driving engagement**

The Chief Marketing Officer ensures that the company's branding, messaging, and campaigns resonate with customer needs. Their responsibilities include:

- leveraging customer data to tailor marketing strategies.
- implementing personalization and loyalty programs.
- ensuring that communication through every channel focuses on customer needs.

**CCO's role: enhancing experience**

The Chief Customer Officer focuses on ensuring seamless and positive customer interactions by:

- developing policies that prioritize customer satisfaction.
- addressing customer pain points through innovation.
- fostering an internal culture where employees understand and advocate for customer needs.

## Case Studies: Putting the Customer First

***Amazon, the gold standard of customer-centricity***

Amazon has built its empire by relentlessly focusing on customer needs. Jeff Bezos, the company's founder, consistently emphasized that the most important single thing is to focus "obsessively" on the customer. Amazon's customer-centric approach is evident in multiple ways:

- **Data-Driven Personalization**: Amazon leverages AI and machine learning to analyze customer preferences, offering personalized product recommendations that enhance shopping experiences.

- **Customer-First Policies**: Amazon Prime, free shipping, hassle-free returns, and a customer-centric refund policy reinforce trust and convenience.

- **Innovation Based on Customer Feedback**: Products like Kindle, Echo, and AWS were developed based on identified customer needs.

- **C-Suite Leadership Commitment**: Amazon's executives continually measure customer satisfaction using key performance indicators such as Net Promoter Score (NPS) and Customer Satisfaction Index (CSI).

***Walt Disney Co., creating magical customer experiences***

Disney exemplifies customer-centricity by designing experiences that exceed customer expectations. From its theme parks to streaming services, Disney's C-suite ensures every aspect of the company revolves around enhancing customer engagement.

- **Commitment to Excellence**: Disney's commitment to superior service is reflected in the Disney Institute's training, which teaches employees to anticipate customer needs proactively.

- **Technological Innovations**: The MagicBand, a wearable device used in Disney parks, enhances guest experiences by allowing seamless entry, purchases, and ride reservations.

- **Emotional Connection**: Disney leverages storytelling and immersive experiences to build strong emotional bonds with customers, increasing brand loyalty.

- **C-Suite Leadership Alignment**: Disney's leadership ensures that customer service is ingrained in company values and that feedback loops inform strategic decisions.

## How Companies Can Implement Customer-Centric Strategies

Organizations can use a number of strategies to build a customer-centric business:

- **Embed Customer-Centricity Into Corporate**

**Culture:** The entire organization, from leadership to frontline employees, must prioritize customer needs.

- **Invest in Technology and Data Analytics:** Leveraging AI, CRM systems, and data analytics enhances customer insights and personalization.
- **Ensure Cross-Functional Collaboration:** All departments work together to ensure a seamless customer experience.
- **Measure Success through Customer Metrics:** Businesses track NPS, Customer Lifetime Value (CLV), and customer retention rates to assess their performance.
- **Continuously Innovate Based on Customer Feedback:** Companies remain agile, adapting to evolving customer preferences and market dynamics.

## Conclusion

Better-managed companies recognize that long-term success depends on a customer-centric strategy. By embedding customer-first thinking into the C-suite's decision-making processes, organizations like Amazon and Disney have set benchmarks in customer experience excellence. As businesses continue to navigate the ever-changing marketplace, those that prioritize customer needs ultimately will thrive, ensuring sustainable growth and enduring brand loyalty.

# Section IV: Protect Your Energy

## Empires Thrive on Efficient Operations

Operational efficiency is a critical factor for businesses that aim to scale revenue and earnings effectively. As companies grow, inefficiencies in processes, cost structures, and resource allocations can become significant obstacles to sustained profitability. By focusing on operational efficiency, organizations can optimize costs, improve productivity, enhance customer satisfaction, and strengthen their competitive advantage.

For small- and mid-cap companies, where resources are often limited, operational efficiency is even more vital. Many smaller firms have successfully scaled by maintaining lean operations and emphasizing strategic cost management.

## The Role of Operational Efficiency in Scaling Businesses

As companies expand, they experience increased complexity in their supply chains, workforce management, and financial operations. Without efficiency measures in place, this complexity can lead to higher costs, reduced agility, and declining margins. The benefits of operational efficiency include:

- **Cost Optimization:** Scaling requires significant

investment in infrastructure, technology, and personnel. Efficient operations help businesses maximize returns on these investments by minimizing waste, automating repetitive tasks, and improving procurement strategies.

- **Revenue Growth Without Proportional Cost Increase:** One of the hallmarks of a well-managed scaling process is revenue growth that outpaces cost growth. Companies that achieve this can reinvest savings into expansion initiatives, research and development, or customer acquisition without eroding profitability.

- **Improved Productivity and Resource Allocation:** Efficiency ensures that employees, capital, and other resources are utilized optimally. This allows companies to do more with less, leading to higher output per unit of input.

- **Enhanced Customer Experience:** Operational efficiency leads to faster turnaround times, improved product or service quality, and more responsive customer support. This can improve customer satisfaction, retention, and brand loyalty.

- **Scalability and Flexibility:** Efficient businesses can scale with fewer growing pains, as streamlined operations allow for quick adaptation to market changes, economic shifts, and evolving consumer demands.

## Key Strategies for Improving Operational Efficiency

- **Automation and Technology Adoption:** Investing in automation tools and enterprise software can significantly enhance efficiency by reducing manual workloads and errors. Cloud computing, AI-driven analytics, and robotic process automation are powerful enablers of operational efficiency.

- **Process Optimization and Lean Operations:** Adopting lean methodologies helps eliminate waste and optimize workflows. Continuous process improvement techniques, such as Six Sigma and Kaizen, can drive efficient gains in production, logistics, and back-office operations.

- **Data-driven Decision Making:** Utilizing analytics to monitor performance and identify bottlenecks allows businesses to make informed decisions that improve efficiency. KPIs should be tracked regularly to assess operational effectiveness.

- **Workforce Optimization and Training:** An engaged and well-trained workforce is essential for maintaining efficiency. Companies should invest in skill development, performance management, and incentive structures that align with business goals.

- **Supply Chain and Vendor Management:** Optimizing supply chains through better inventory management, strategic partnerships, and demand forecasting can lead to cost savings and improved service levels.

## Case Studies: Small-Caps Focused on Operational Efficiency

***The Lovesac Co.***

Lovesac, a small-cap furniture company specializing in modular seating, demonstrated exceptional operational efficiency. Despite operating in a capital-intensive industry, Lovesac achieved impressive revenue growth by:

- utilizing an innovative supply chain model that reduced inventory risk.

- leveraging e-commerce and direct-to-consumer sales channels to minimize brick-and-mortar costs.

- implementing lean manufacturing techniques to improve production efficiency and reduce waste.

Lovesac's focus on asset-light operations and strategic cost management enabled it to scale without incurring unsustainable overhead costs, leading to strong profitability.

***Axon Enterprise Inc.***

Axon, known for its body cameras and law enforcement technology, leveraged operational efficiency to drive growth. The company focused on:

- automating its production processes to maintain high product quality while reducing costs.
- implementing a software-as-a-service (SaaS) model for digital evidence management, creating a recurring revenue stream with high margins.
- using data analytics to optimize inventory levels and enhance demand forecasting.

By continuously refining its operations and adopting cutting-edge technology, Axon scaled efficiently and maintained strong earnings growth.

## Conclusion

For companies looking to scale revenue and earnings, operational efficiency is a necessity. Businesses that focus on optimizing costs, leveraging technology, streamlining processes, and making data-driven decisions are better positioned for long-term success. Small-cap companies like Lovesac and Axon Enterprise demonstrate that a commitment to efficiency can lead to substantial growth and competitive advantage.

As organizations navigate the complexities of scaling, prioritizing operational efficiency allows them to maintain profitability, enhance customer experiences, and sustain a trajectory of growth.

# Section V: The Power of Passion and Energy

## Attract Customers by Investing in the Vision

Companies that aspire to grow their revenue, brands, and earnings must harness passion and energy at every level, especially in the C-suite. Passion and energy fuel innovation, drive strategic execution, and create a company culture that inspires employees and customers alike. Without them, businesses risk stagnation, losing market share to competitors who operate with greater enthusiasm and determination.

Small- and mid-cap companies often face the challenge of scaling efficiently while maintaining their agility. Companies such as Crocs Inc. and Deckers Outdoor Corp. exemplify how passion and energy in the C-suite can translate into brand expansion, revenue growth, and increased earnings.

## The Role of Passion in Business Growth

Passion is a driving force that transforms ordinary companies into extraordinary brands. When leaders are deeply invested in their company's vision, they create a sense of purpose that resonates throughout the organization.

**Passion as a competitive advantage.**

Passionate leaders do not simply manage businesses—they inspire them. They bring excitement and commitment to their roles, which fosters a culture of excellence and innovation. This is particularly important in small- and mid-cap companies that need to differentiate themselves from larger competitors.

A prime example is Crocs Inc., a global leader in innovative casual footwear. Over the years, Crocs transformed from a niche footwear brand into a global powerhouse by embracing its unique product design and engaging with its passionate customer base. CEO Andrew Rees and his leadership team demonstrated unwavering enthusiasm for the brand, leveraging creative collaborations, celebrity endorsements, and digital engagement strategies that drove a significant revenue increase.

**Passion drives innovation and growth.**

When leaders are passionate about their business, they actively seek out new opportunities for expansion. Passionate executives are not afraid to take bold risks, experiment with new ideas, and embrace change.

For instance, Deckers Outdoor Corp., owner of popular brands such as UGG, HOKA, and Teva, harnessed its leadership's passion for premium footwear and transformed UGG into a fashion statement rather than just a cold-weather boot. Under CEO Dave Powers, the company also aggressively expanded

HOKA, a high-performance athletic shoe brand, positioning it as a leader in the running shoe industry. Deckers' passion for brand differentiation and quality innovation helped the company significantly grow its revenue and market share.

**Passion enhances brand identity and customer loyalty.**

Customers are drawn to companies that exude passion. Whether it's through product design, marketing campaigns, or corporate values, passion creates a deeper connection with consumers.

Crocs exemplifies this concept by turning what was once a polarizing footwear choice into a beloved brand with a cult following. The company's passion for self-expression and individuality is reflected in its limited-edition collaborations, social media engagement, and strategic partnerships with global influencers. This passion translates into brand loyalty, leading to repeat customers and higher revenue.

## The Role of Energy in Business Leadership

While passion sets the vision, energy is what drives execution. Energy ensures that strategic goals are met, employees remain engaged, and momentum is sustained over time.

**Energy fuels a high-performance culture.**

A leader's energy is contagious. When executives bring enthusiasm and dynamism to their roles, employees respond with increased motivation and productivity. Energy creates a workplace where employees feel inspired to contribute their best efforts.

Deckers Outdoor Corp. cultivated a high-energy culture that encourages innovation and agility. By investing in sustainable practices, supply chain efficiency, and product expansion, the company continues to push forward with momentum. The leadership team made a habit of engaging with employees, fostering a culture where ideas are shared, risks are encouraged, and execution is swift.

**Energy drives execution and resilience.**

Growing a business requires relentless effort, particularly in dynamic markets. Leaders with high energy levels ensure that strategies are not only developed but also executed with precision. They set ambitious goals, hold teams accountable, and maintain a sense of urgency that prevents stagnation.

Crocs Inc. demonstrated this principle through its rapid international expansion and digital transformation. Instead of resting on past successes, Crocs' leadership team pushed forward with aggressive marketing strategies, expanded e-commerce operations, and strengthened its direct-to-consumer channels. Their energy in executing these initiatives resulted in record-breaking sales and market penetration.

**Energy sustains long-term growth.**

A company's ability to sustain growth depends on how well it maintains its energy over time. Leaders who consistently bring enthusiasm to their work inspire longevity and resilience within their organizations.

Deckers Outdoor Corp. showcased how sustained energy can lead to long-term success. With a strong focus on sustainability, digital transformation, and brand evolution, Deckers continued to evolve without losing momentum. CEO Powers and his team demonstrated how staying energized and committed to long-term strategies can lead to compounding revenue and earnings growth.

## How Companies Embed Passion and Energy Into the Culture

Passion and energy cannot be limited to the C-suite; they must be woven into the fabric of the company culture, regardless of the size. Here's how companies can cultivate these qualities to drive growth:

**Hire leaders who embody passion and energy.**

Companies must be intentional about selecting executives who bring genuine excitement and dynamism to their roles. When hiring or promoting leaders, organizations should prioritize candidates who exhibit a deep connection to the company's mission and a strong drive to execute bold strategies.

**Foster a purpose-driven culture.**

Employees are more engaged when they believe in what they are working toward. Companies should establish a compelling mission statement, reinforce their core values, and create a sense of shared purpose among employees. When a company has a clear "why," employees and customers alike will rally behind it.

**Encourage innovation and experimentation.**

Passionate and energetic leaders create environments where employees feel safe to take risks, pitch new ideas, and challenge the status quo. Encouraging innovation ensures that companies remain competitive and continuously evolve.

**Communicate enthusiasm across all levels.**

Leaders should actively communicate their excitement about the company's future through regular town halls, strategy meetings, and open discussions. When employees see executives who are deeply engaged, they are more likely to be inspired and motivated.

**Celebrate wins and maintain momentum.**

Sustaining energy within a company requires recognizing and celebrating achievements. Whether it's reaching revenue milestones, launching a successful product, or hitting brand engagement targets, acknowledging progress keeps employees motivated and reinforces a culture of achievement.

## Conclusion

Passion and energy are essential ingredients for any company seeking to grow its revenue, brands, and earnings. Leaders who bring these qualities to their roles inspire innovation, drive execution, and cultivate a culture of high performance.

Mid-cap companies like Crocs Inc. and Deckers Outdoor Corp. illustrate how a leadership team infused with passion and energy can transform a business into a global powerhouse. Their commitment to brand identity, customer engagement, and operational excellence resulted in sustained revenue growth and market success.

Organizations looking to scale can embed passion and energy into leadership positions and company culture. By hiring visionary leaders, fostering a purpose-driven culture, and maintaining an unwavering commitment to execution, companies can achieve long-term financial success while making a lasting impact on their industry.

# 6

# Play the Game at the Highest Level

*Make Bold Moves, Create Value.*

## Section I: Speak the Language of Money

### If You Can't Read the Numbers, You Can't Lead

Financial management is a fundamental responsibility for executives in the C-suite. Whether a company is a small-cap business striving to scale revenue and earnings or a well-established enterprise looking to optimize financial performance, understanding core financial principles is essential. Strong financial leadership ensures sustainability, profitability, and strategic growth.

C-suite executives, particularly CEOs, CFOs, and COOs, must have a deep understanding of financial management. This includes interpreting financial statements, managing budgets, controlling costs, and making data-driven decisions. Without financial literacy, even the most promising businesses can struggle with cash flow, misallocated resources, or inefficient operations.

## The Importance of Financial Management in the C-Suite

Executives in the C-suite must oversee financial performance to ensure sustainable business growth and profitability. Without effective financial management, executives can't determine the best moves for their companies. Effective financial management enables leaders to:

- make informed decisions based on accurate financial data.
- allocate resources efficiently to maximize ROI.
- optimize revenue streams while maintaining cost control.
- improve profitability and shareholder value.
- manage risks and economic uncertainties.

## Key Areas of Financial Management in the C-Suite

To achieve financial success, executives must understand the following critical areas:

**Budgets and financial planning**

A budget is a financial road map that guides a company's income and expenditures over a specific period. Executives use budgets to set spending limits, allocate resources, and measure financial performance against business objectives.

The role of the C-suite in budgeting:

- CEOs and CFOs oversee budget planning, ensuring alignment with strategic goals.
- COOs manage operational costs and resource allocation.
- CMOs and sales leaders forecast revenue and marketing expenses.

Key budgeting components:

- Revenue projections – estimating expected income from various revenue streams
- Fixed vs. variable costs – fixed expenses hold steady (e.g., rent, salaries) while variable expenses go up or down regularly (e.g., raw materials, marketing)
- Capital expenditures – investments in infrastructure, technology, and long-term assets
- Operating expenses – day-to-day costs
- Cash flow forecasting – ensuring that sufficient cash reserves are available

Best practices for budgeting:

- Use historical data and industry benchmarks to set realistic budgets.

- Implement rolling forecasts to adjust budgets based on real-time performance.
- Ensure budgets align with strategic growth initiatives.

## Understanding revenue streams and growth strategies

Revenue is the lifeblood of a business. C-suite executives must identify, optimize, and diversify revenue streams to drive financial stability and growth.

Types of revenue streams:

- Product sales – direct sales of goods or services
- Subscription models – recurring revenue from memberships or software licensing.
- Advertising and sponsorships – monetizing media, digital platforms, or brand partnerships
- Licensing and royalties – generating income from intellectual property or brand use
- Consulting and services – offering expertise in exchange for fees

Revenue optimization strategies:

- Market expansion – entering new geographical markets or customer segments

- Product diversification – developing new offerings to meet consumer demand

- Pricing strategy – optimizing pricing to maximize margins without losing customers

- Customer retention – increasing customer lifetime value (LTV) through loyalty programs and personalized marketing

Example: Sarah Kauss, founder and former CEO of S'well:

- Built a premium water bottle brand with strong revenue growth by differentiating in a competitive market.

- Expanded revenue streams by partnering with luxury brands and launching custom collaborations.

- Scaled the business by investing in direct-to-consumer sales and e-commerce.

## Understanding the profit and loss (P&L) statement

The P&L statement, also called an income statement, provides a snapshot of a company's revenues, expenses, and profitability over a specific period.

Key components of the P&L statement:

- Revenue (top line) – total income generated from sales and services

- Cost of goods sold (COGS) – direct costs of producing goods or services
- Gross profit – revenue minus COGS, showing profitability before overhead costs
- Operating expenses – includes salaries, rent, utilities, and marketing expenses
- EBITDA (Earnings Before Interest, Taxes, Depreciation, and Amortization) – measures operational profitability
- Net income (bottom line) – profit after all expenses, taxes, and interest

How the C-suite uses the P&L statement:

- CEOs and CFOs assess financial health and identify trends in profitability.
- COOs optimize operational efficiency to improve gross profit margins.
- CMOs evaluate the impact of marketing expenditures on revenue growth.

Example: Patrick Spence, CEO of Sonos:

- Used financial analyses to optimize pricing and margins.
- Invested in direct-to-consumer channels to improve revenue streams.

- Managed costs effectively, driving profitability while expanding market share.

### Cost controls and expense management

Controlling costs is crucial for maximizing profitability. C-suite executives must ensure that spending aligns with business priorities and delivers a strong return on investment.

Key cost-control strategies:

- Lean operations – reduce waste and improve efficiency
- Vendor negotiations – secure better pricing from suppliers
- Process automation – use technology to reduce manual work and operational costs
- Workforce optimization – balance hiring needs with cost efficiency

Managing fixed vs. variable costs:

- Fixed costs – rent, insurance, long-term contracts
- Variable costs – marketing expenses, raw materials, commissions

Role of the C-suite in cost control:

- CFOs develop policies to monitor and control expenditures.

- COOs identify inefficiencies in supply chain and logistics.
- CEOs ensure cost control aligns with business objectives.

Example: Tom Gimbel, CEO of LaSalle Network

- Scaled a staffing firm by proactively managing operational costs.
- Implemented technology to streamline recruitment, reducing overhead.
- Focused on employee retention to minimize hiring and training costs.

**Understanding the balance sheet**

The balance sheet provides a snapshot of a company's financial position at a specific point in time. It includes assets, liabilities, and shareholders' equity.

Key sections of the balance sheet:

- Assets:

  a. Current assets – cash, accounts receivable, inventory

  b. Fixed assets – property, equipment, intellectual property

- Liabilities:

    a. Current liabilities – short-term debts, accounts payable

    b. Long-term liabilities – loans, bonds, pension obligations

    c. Shareholders' equity, or the retained earnings and capital invested by shareholders

**How the C-suite Uses the Balance Sheet:**

- Liquidity management – ensuring enough cash reserves for operations

- Debt vs. equity decisions – balancing funding sources for expansion

- Investment strategy – allocating capital effectively

- Example: Katrina Lake, founder and former CEO of Stitch Fix:

- Used balance sheet analysis to manage cash flow and optimize inventory levels.

- Scaled business while maintaining financial discipline.

- Focused on profitability through data-driven operations.

## Conclusion

Financial management is a critical competency for C-suite executives, influencing decision-making, growth strategies, and long-term sustainability. A strong grasp of budgeting, revenue streams, profit and loss statements, cost control, and balance sheets allows leaders to make informed, strategic choices.

Executives like Patrick Spence and Katrina Lake exemplify how financial acumen can drive small-cap companies toward scalable revenue growth and earnings. Tom Gimbel consistently used financial data to assess risk exposures and safeguard his hedge fund customers' assets. Sarah Kauss strategically reinvested revenue into growth initiatives that reinforced her brand's vision. By mastering these financial principles, the C-suite can navigate complexities, mitigate risks, and optimize business performance for sustained success.

# Section II: Trust the Data, Not the Drama

## Insight Wins Over Instinct

In any organization, leaders must leverage data to drive strategic decision-making. The C-suite plays a critical role in shaping a company's future. Data-driven decision-making enables these leaders to make informed choices that lead to sustainable growth, increased profitability, and enhanced customer satisfaction.

## Why Organizations Must Be Data-Driven

Data-driven organizations make decisions based on insights derived from accurate and relevant data, rather than relying solely on intuition or historical experiences. Here are some key reasons why organizations should adopt a data-driven approach:

**Improved decision-making accuracy**

Data-driven decision-making minimizes bias and subjectivity, ensuring that choices are based on objective insights and evidence. Executives who rely on data can identify patterns, trends, and correlations that would otherwise go unnoticed. For example, predictive analytics can help businesses anticipate market shifts, allowing them to adjust their strategies proactively.

**Enhanced competitive advantage**

Organizations that leverage data effectively gain a significant competitive edge. Companies like Amazon and Google have demonstrated how data analytics can optimize customer experiences, streamline operations, and drive innovation. Businesses that fail to adopt data-driven strategies risk being outperformed by competitors who do.

### Increased operational efficiency

By analyzing data, organizations can identify inefficiencies, reduce costs, and improve productivity. Data analytics can help with workforce management, supply chain optimization, and financial forecasting, all of which contribute to improved operational performance.

### Better customer insights and personalization

Understanding customer behavior and preferences is crucial for business success. Data analytics enables organizations to segment their customer base, predict purchasing behaviors, and deliver personalized experiences. This approach improves customer satisfaction and fosters long-term loyalty.

### Risk mitigation and fraud detection

Data-driven decision-making enhances risk management by enabling organizations to detect anomalies, predict potential risks, and implement preventive measures. Financial institutions, for instance, use data analytics to detect fraudulent transactions and mitigate cyber threats.

## The Role of the C-Suite in Data-Driven Decision Making

While data-driven decision-making benefits organizations as a whole, its impact is most profound when embraced at the executive level. C-suite executives must champion a culture of data-driven decision-making to ensure alignment across all departments.

**Chief Executive Officer**

Data-driven CEOs leverage analytics to:

- define long-term business strategies.
- monitor key performance indicators (KPIs).
- identify new market opportunities.
- enhance investor relations through data transparency.

**Chief Financial Officer**

Data-driven CFOs use analytics for:

- real-time financial reporting.
- budget forecasting and expense tracking.
- investment analysis and decision-making.

### Chief Marketing Officer

Marketing decisions must be supported by data to ensure optimal ROI. CMOs utilize data analytics to:

- understand customer segmentation and demographics.
- optimize marketing campaigns based on real-time feedback.
- track conversion rates and measure marketing effectiveness.

### Chief Data Officer

A relatively new role in many organizations, the CDO is responsible for data governance, data quality, and implementing analytics strategies across the company.

## Case Studies: CEOs Who Have Embraced the Data

***Jeff Bezos, Amazon***

Jeff Bezos, the founder and former CEO of Amazon, built the company into one of the world's most valuable enterprises by prioritizing data and analytics. Bezos leveraged data-driven decision-making in various aspects of Amazon's operations, including:

- **Customer Experience:** Amazon's recommendation

engine, powered by AI and data analytics, drives a sizable portion of its revenue by personalizing product suggestions for customers.

- **Operational Efficiency:** Amazon uses predictive analytics for inventory management, ensuring optimal stock levels while reducing waste and inefficiencies.

- **Pricing Strategies:** The company continuously analyzes competitor pricing and customer behavior to adjust prices dynamically, maintaining a competitive edge.

By embedding data-driven culture into Amazon's DNA, Bezos transformed the company into a global leader in e-commerce and cloud computing.

***Satya Nadella, Microsoft***

Satya Nadella is another exemplary leader who has demonstrated the power of data-driven decision-making. Nadella transformed Microsoft into a cloud-first, AI-driven organization. Key initiatives under his leadership include:

- **Azure Cloud Growth:** Nadella's data-driven approach led to Microsoft's shift toward cloud computing, which now generates significant revenue.

- **AI and Machine Learning Integration:** Microsoft embedded AI and analytics into its products, including Office 365, Dynamics 365, and LinkedIn, providing businesses with intelligent insights.

- **Customer-Centric Strategy:** Microsoft uses data analytics to understand customer needs, enhance user experience, and develop innovative solutions tailored to different industries.

Through his leadership, Nadella positioned Microsoft as a dominant force in the technology sector by leveraging data to drive strategic decisions.

## Challenges to Implementing Data-Driven Decision-Making

Despite its advantages, adopting a data-driven approach comes with challenges:

**Data Silos and Integration Issues:** Many organizations struggle with fragmented data systems that hinder access to unified insights. Executives must invest in integrating data from various sources to ensure a holistic view.

**Data Quality and Governance:** Poor data quality can lead to inaccurate insights and misguided decisions. Organizations need robust data governance policies to ensure accuracy, consistency, and security.

**Cultural Resistance to Change:** Shifting to a data-driven culture requires a mindset change at all levels. Resistance to data adoption often stems from a lack of understanding or fear of modern technologies. Strong leadership is essential to drive this transition.

**Cybersecurity and Data Privacy Concerns:** With increased data utilization comes the risk of breaches and privacy issues.

Organizations must implement stringent cybersecurity measures and comply with regulations like the General Data Protection Regulation (GDPR) and the California Consumer Privacy Act (CCPA).

## Conclusion

The importance of data-driven decision-making in the C-suite cannot be overstated. Organizations that harness the power of data gain a significant competitive advantage, improve operational efficiency, enhance customer experiences, and mitigate risks. CEOs like Jeff Bezos and Satya Nadella demonstrated how leveraging data can lead to groundbreaking success.

To thrive in the digital age, companies must cultivate a data-driven culture, invest in analytics tools, and empower executives with the insights needed to make informed strategic decisions. By doing so, organizations can position themselves for long-term growth, profitability, and market leadership.

# Section III: Negotiate Like a Closer

## Every Big Leap Is Earned at the Table

Scaling a company successfully requires more than just an excellent product or service. One of the most critical skills an entrepreneur or executive must possess is the ability to negotiate and make strategic deals. Negotiation and deal-making are the backbone of business growth, enabling companies to secure partnerships, attract investment, optimize cost structures, and gain competitive advantages. Effective negotiation can be the difference between a company stagnating and one growing exponentially.

## The Role of Negotiation in Business Scaling

### Securing strategic partnerships

Partnerships are crucial when scaling a company, as they provide access to new markets, technologies, and distribution channels. Negotiating favorable terms in partnerships ensures that both parties benefit while minimizing risks. Strategic alliances can reduce operational costs, increase brand credibility, and offer mutually beneficial growth opportunities.

For instance, when Steve Jobs negotiated with Microsoft in 1997 to secure a $150 million investment in Apple, he not only ensured Apple's survival but also laid the foundation for its future dominance. His ability to strike a deal with a direct competitor demonstrated his negotiation prowess and vision.

### Attracting investment and funding

Scaling requires capital, and securing that investment involves negotiating terms with venture capitalists, private equity firms, or financial institutions. Entrepreneurs must be adept at articulating their company's value proposition, addressing investor concerns, and ensuring they retain sufficient control over their business.

Elon Musk, the CEO of Tesla and SpaceX, is known for his ability to negotiate high-stakes deals with investors. His negotiations with government agencies and private investors have enabled Tesla and SpaceX to secure billions in funding, leading to rapid growth and industry disruption.

### Negotiating customer and supplier agreements

Strong relationships with suppliers and customers are essential for scalability. Negotiating favorable terms with suppliers can lead to cost savings, better payment terms, and improved supply chain efficiency. Similarly, negotiating long-term contracts with customers ensures revenue stability and strengthens market position.

For example, Amazon, under Bezos's leadership, negotiated aggressively with suppliers and logistics partners to secure lower prices and favorable shipping rates for Amazon products. These negotiations allowed Amazon to offer competitive prices while maintaining healthy profit margins, fueling its exponential growth.

### Hiring and retaining top talent

Scaling a business requires attracting and retaining top talent. Salary negotiations, equity distribution, and benefits packages must be structured to appeal to high-caliber professionals while maintaining financial sustainability.

Reed Hastings, the co-founder and CEO of Netflix, is known for his innovative approach to talent negotiations. By offering employees high salaries and a culture of freedom and responsibility, he has attracted top talent, allowing Netflix to scale into a global entertainment powerhouse.

### Navigating mergers and acquisitions

Mergers and acquisitions (M&A) are often essential for scaling, providing companies with access to new markets, technologies, and talent. Successful negotiations in M&A transactions require strategic foresight, due diligence, and effective communication.

One of the most notable examples of M&A negotiation is Disney's acquisition of Pixar. Bob Iger, Disney's CEO at the time, skillfully negotiated the $7.4 billion deal, securing the collaboration of Steve Jobs and Pixar's leadership. This acquisition revitalized Disney's animation division and significantly contributed to its growth.

## Key Principles of Effective Negotiation

**Preparation and Research:** Successful negotiators conduct thorough research to understand their counterparts' motivations, pain points, and goals. This information enables them to craft compelling proposals and anticipate objections.

**Win-Win Mentality:** Successful negotiation does not mean one party wins while the other loses. The most effective deals create value for both parties, fostering long-term relationships and sustainable growth.

**Effective Communication:** Clarity, active listening, and persuasive storytelling are essential negotiation skills. Negotiators must articulate their value proposition convincingly while addressing concerns and building trust.

**Flexibility and Adaptability:** Business negotiations are dynamic, requiring negotiators to adapt their strategies based on the latest information, shifting market conditions, and evolving stakeholder priorities.

**Emotional Intelligence and Patience:** Emotional intelligence helps negotiators manage stress, understand the emotions of others, and build rapport. Patience is equally crucial, as the best deals often take time to finalize.

## Case Studies: CEOs Who Mastered Negotiation

### ***Elon Musk, Tesla and SpaceX***

Elon Musk's negotiation skills played a pivotal role in Tesla and SpaceX securing government contracts, attracting high-profile investors, and forming strategic partnerships. For example:

- Musk negotiated with the state of Nevada to secure $1.3 billion in incentives for Tesla's Gigafactory. This deal was critical in Tesla's battery production and electric vehicle expansion.

- Musk successfully negotiated multi-billion-dollar contracts with NASA, positioning SpaceX as a leader in space exploration.

***Jeff Bezos, Amazon***

Jeff Bezos transformed Amazon from an online bookstore into a trillion-dollar empire through masterful negotiations. His approach included:

- negotiating aggressively with book publishers and suppliers to secure the lowest prices, ensuring Amazon's competitive edge.

- engaging in strategic negotiations to secure major corporate and government clients for Amazon Web Services, fueling the company's revenue growth.

***Bob Iger, Disney***

Bob Iger's negotiation expertise contributed significantly to Disney's growth through acquisitions.

- Iger convinced Apple's Steve Jobs to sell Pixar to Disney, revitalizing Disney's animation division.

- By acquiring Marvel ($4 billion) and Lucasfilm ($4 billion), Iger expanded Disney's intellectual property portfolio, leading to blockbuster franchises like the Marvel Cinematic Universe and Star Wars sequels.

## Conclusion

Negotiation and deal-making are indispensable skills for scaling a company. From securing strategic partnerships and funding to hiring top talent and navigating mergers, negotiation influences every aspect of business growth. Leaders like Elon Musk, Jeff Bezos, and Bob Iger exemplify how strategic negotiation can propel a company to unprecedented success.

For entrepreneurs and executives looking to scale their businesses, mastering negotiation techniques is essential. By prioritizing preparation, communication, adaptability, and emotional intelligence, they can drive sustainable growth and achieve long-term success regardless of the competition.

# Section IV: Lead Big Moves

## Growth Requires Guts and Guidance

No matter what the industry, companies face constant pressure to grow, innovate, and stay competitive. One of the most effective ways to achieve these goals is through mergers and acquisitions. M&A transactions can drive market expansion, diversify product lines, and create operational efficiencies. However, these deals carry significant risks, requiring leaders with the right expertise to navigate them successfully. This is why having M&A experience in the C-suite is an essential criterion for corporate leadership.

## The Role of M&A in Corporate Growth and Strategy

M&A transactions are strategic tools that companies use to achieve a variety of objectives, including:

- **Market Expansion:** Acquiring companies in new geographic markets can provide instant access to customer bases and distribution networks.

- **Product and Service Diversification:** Companies can quickly expand their offerings by acquiring businesses with complementary products.

- **Operational Synergies:** Mergers can lead to cost reductions through economies of scale, supply chain integration, and workforce optimization.

- **Technology and Innovation Access:** Acquiring startups and innovative firms can accelerate a company's technological advancements.

- **Competitive Positioning:** M&A can help a company outpace rivals by consolidating market share or acquiring strategic intellectual property.

## The Necessity of M&A Expertise in the C-Suite

Given the high stakes of M&A, executives must possess a deep understanding of deal structuring, due diligence, integration strategies, and risk mitigation. The following roles within the C-suite particularly benefit from M&A experience:

### Chief Executive Officer

M&A expertise enables a CEO to:

- identify and evaluate potential acquisition targets that align with corporate objectives.
- communicate a clear vision of how acquisitions fit into the company's growth strategy.
- lead integration efforts to ensure a seamless transition after the merger.
- gain investor confidence by demonstrating a proven history of value-creating acquisitions.

### Chief Financial Officer

The CFO oversees financial due diligence, valuation, and deal structuring during a merger or acquisition. M&A experience helps the CFO:

- accurately assess the financial health of target companies.
- optimize deal financing through debt, equity, or hybrid structures.
- manage post-acquisition financial reporting and risk assessment.
- identify cost structures and revenue opportunities that maximize deal value.

**Chief Operating Officer**

The COO ensures that the acquired companies are integrated smoothly into the existing organization. M&A experience allows a COO to:

- develop operational strategies for merging company cultures, processes, and supply chains.
- mitigate risks associated with workforce consolidation and reorganization.
- align newly acquired teams with corporate goals and KPIs.

## Case Studies: Mid-Cap CEOs with M&A Success

***Brent Yeagy, Wabash***

Wabash is a mid-cap leader in the transportation and logistics industry, manufacturing truck and trailer solutions. Under CEO Brent Yeagy's leadership, the company executed strategic acquisitions to expand into high-growth market segments. For example, Wabash acquired Supreme Industries to enter the final-mile delivery market, capitalizing on the e-commerce boom. Yeagy's M&A strategy helped Wabash diversify its revenue streams, strengthen supply chain capabilities, and maintain a competitive edge.

***Tom Priore, Priority Technology Holdings***

Priority Technology Holdings operates in the payments and banking-as-a-service sector. CEO Tom Priore strategically used M&A to consolidate fintech solutions, allowing the company to enhance its product offerings and customer base. Through well-planned acquisitions, Priority Technology Holdings expanded its payment processing infrastructure, enabling the company to scale rapidly and compete with larger players in the industry. Priore's ability to structure and integrate acquisitions effectively was instrumental in the company's growth trajectory.

## Seeking Leadership With M&A Experience

For companies considering M&A as a growth strategy, ensuring that the leadership team has direct experience in deal-making is critical. Organizations should:

- prioritize M&A experience when hiring or promoting executives in the C-suite.

- provide training and mentorship opportunities to develop M&A expertise among senior leaders.

- leverage external advisors or board members with M&A backgrounds to supplement internal knowledge.

## Conclusion

Today's corporate leaders must have M&A experience. The ability to identify, execute, and integrate strategic acquisitions can separate a company from its competitors and drive long-term success. As demonstrated by leaders like Brent Yeagy and Tom Priore, CEOs with M&A acumen can create substantial value for shareholders and position their organizations for sustained growth.

# 7

# Command the Room and the Boardroom

*Earn Influence Where It Matters Most*

## Section I: Lead Stakeholders, Don't Chase Them.

### When They Know Where You're Going, They'll Willingly Follow

Effective stakeholder management is a critical competency for the C-suite of any company. Whether it is the CEO, CFO, CHRO, or any other executive, engaging effectively with key stakeholders is essential for sustained business success. These stakeholders may include board members, investors, employees, customers, suppliers, and the broader community, and together they influence the company's financial performance, strategic direction, brand reputation, and overall stability.

## Understanding Stakeholders

Stakeholders can be broadly categorized into two groups:

- **Internal Stakeholders:** Employees, executives, board members, and company leadership.
- **External Stakeholders:** Investors, customers, suppliers, regulators, and the broader community.

Each group has distinct priorities and expectations. Managing these diverse interests requires a structured approach that aligns with corporate goals while maintaining strong relationships with all parties involved.

## Why Stakeholder Engagement is Essential

### Enhancing corporate governance and board relations

Board members provide oversight, strategic guidance, and accountability. The C-suite must engage with the board transparently and regularly to ensure alignment on key issues such as business strategy, risk management, and financial performance.

Effective stakeholder engagement:

- ensures clarity in corporate governance.
- strengthens strategic alignment between leadership and the board.

- builds trust and credibility through transparent communication.

- facilitates smoother decision-making and long-term planning.

## Investor relations and financial stability

Investors, including shareholders and private equity firms, have a vested interest in a company's performance. Effective communication and engagement help maintain their confidence and secure financial support for growth initiatives.

When done well, this communication:

- increases investor confidence and trust.

- enhances the company's ability to secure funding for expansion.

- reduces the risk of shareholder activism and hostile takeovers.

- supports better stock performance and valuation.

## Employee engagement and retention

Employees are the backbone of any organization. Strong leadership that listens to and addresses employee concerns fosters a positive work environment, enhances job satisfaction, and boosts productivity.

Keeping employees up to date:

- improves morale and job satisfaction.
- increases retention rates and reduces turnover costs.
- enhances productivity and innovation.
- strengthens the brand, making attracting top talent easier.

**Customer and market trust**

Customers are the company's primary revenue source. Engaging with customers to understand their needs, concerns, and feedback helps improve products and services, ultimately leading to increased customer satisfaction and loyalty.

Engaging with customers:

- strengthens brand reputation and customer trust.
- increases customer retention and lifetime value.
- provides insights into product and service innovation.
- enhances competitive advantage in the market.

## Supplier and partner relations

Suppliers and business partners are critical for supply chain efficiency and operational success. Fostering strong relationships ensures reliability, better pricing, and access to new business opportunities.

Maintaining positive supplier and partner relationships:

- enhances supply chain resilience.
- improves cost efficiency and quality assurance.
- encourages strategic collaboration and innovation.
- reduces the risk of disruptions and delays.

## Regulatory compliance and public affairs

Regulators and government bodies shape the legal and operational framework within which a company operates. Proactively engaging with these stakeholders helps the organization remain compliant with laws, avoid legal issues, and influence policy decisions beneficial to the industry.

Positive relationships with regulators and government entities:

- ensures regulatory compliance and reduces legal risks.
- improves relationships with government and industry bodies.

- enhances corporate social responsibility initiatives.
- positions the company as a responsible corporate citizen.

## Strategies for Effective Stakeholder Management

### Develop a stakeholder engagement plan.

A structured plan helps identify key stakeholders, assess their influence, and develop tailored engagement strategies.

Key steps:

1. Identify key stakeholders and categorize them based on influence and interest.
2. Establish clear objectives for engagement.
3. Assign responsibilities to leadership for maintaining relationships.
4. Measure engagement effectiveness and adjust strategies accordingly.

### Prioritize transparent communication.

Honest and regular communication fosters trust and reduces misunderstandings.

Best practices:

- Hold regular meetings with the board and investors.
- Use multiple channels (e.g., town halls, reports, one-on-one meetings) to communicate with employees.
- Provide timely updates on business performance and strategy.
- Maintain open dialogue with regulatory bodies and policymakers.

**Foster collaboration and inclusivity.**

Engaging stakeholders in decision-making creates a sense of ownership and alignment with corporate goals.

How to implement:

- Involve employees in strategic discussions through surveys and feedback sessions.
- Include investors and board members in planning for the long term.
- Develop joint initiatives with suppliers and partners to drive mutual benefits.

**Leverage technology and data analytics.**

Using data-driven insights allows executives to monitor stakeholder sentiment and make informed decisions.

Tech tools:

- Customer Relationship Management (CRM) software for tracking customer and partner interactions.
- Employee engagement platforms to gather real-time feedback.
- Investor relations dashboards for financial performance tracking.
- Social listening tools to monitor brand perception in the market.

**Build crisis management and contingency plans.**

Proactive crisis management strengthens relationships by demonstrating accountability and preparedness.

Key actions:

- Develop clear crisis communication protocols.
- Establish a crisis response team within the organization.
- Engage with stakeholders early and transparently during crises.

- Learn from past crises and continuously improve response strategies.

## Case Studies: Successful Stakeholder Management

***Apple Inc., board and investor relations***

Apple has consistently maintained strong relationships with its board and investors through clear communication, strategic leadership, and robust financial performance. The company regularly updates stakeholders on new innovations, market trends, and long-term goals, reinforcing trust and stability.

***Google (Alphabet), employee engagement***

Google's emphasis on employee well-being and engagement positioned it as a top employer. By prioritizing open communication, career development programs, and workplace flexibility, Google has maintained high retention rates and continues to attract top talent.

***Tesla, customer-centric innovation***

Tesla actively engages with customers through social media, direct communication, and customer feedback loops. This approach helps the company stay ahead of industry trends and continuously improve its products.

## Conclusion

Stakeholder management is a fundamental responsibility of the C-suite. Engaging proactively with board members, investors, employees, customers, and other key stakeholders fosters trust, drives financial success, and ensures long-term sustainability. By implementing structured engagement strategies, leveraging technology, and maintaining transparent communication, companies can strengthen stakeholder relationships and position themselves for long-term growth and success.

## Section II: Own the Boardroom

### Earn Trust Where Decisions Are Made

The relationship between the C-suite and the corporate Board of Directors is a critical factor in the success of any organization. Effective collaboration fosters strategic alignment, enhances corporate governance, and drives sustainable growth. When the dynamics of this relationship are solid, companies flourish.

### Responsibilities of the C-Suite

The C-suite, led by the CEO, is responsible for the day-to-day operations of the company. Key responsibilities include:

- **Strategic Planning and Execution:** Developing and implementing corporate strategy.

- **Financial Oversight:** Managing the company's financial health.

- **Operational Management:** Overseeing core business functions and ensuring efficiency.

- **Risk Management:** Identifying and mitigating risks to the organization.

- **Culture and Leadership Development:** Building a strong corporate culture and leadership pipeline.

## Responsibilities of the Board of Directors

The Board of Directors provides oversight, ensuring that the company is managed in a manner that aligns with shareholder interests. Key responsibilities include:

- **Corporate Governance:** Establishing policies and ensuring compliance.

- **Executive Oversight:** Hiring, evaluating, and, if necessary, replacing the CEO.

- **Strategic Guidance:** Providing insights and approving major corporate decisions.

- **Risk Oversight:** Assessing and mitigating risks associated with company operations.

- **Financial Stewardship:** Approving budgets and monitoring financial performance.

## Key Principles for a Strong Relationship

To build a productive partnership, both the C-suite and the Board must adhere to core principles:

**Transparency and open communication**

- CEOs and senior executives should provide regular and honest updates on the company's performance, challenges, and opportunities.
- Board members should have access to all relevant information to make informed decisions.
- Regular meetings, reports, and informal touchpoints can strengthen this transparency.

**Strategic alignment**

- The board and C-suite must be aligned on the long-term vision and objectives of the company.
- Strategic discussions should be collaborative, with input from executives and directors.
- Executives should seek feedback from board members on key initiatives.

### Mutual trust and respect

- The C-suite and the board should cultivate an environment of trust where each party respects the expertise and role of the other.
- Board members should not micromanage but should provide strategic oversight.
- The C-suite should be open to board recommendations and guidance.

### Defined roles and responsibilities

- Clearly delineating roles prevents overreach and confusion, ensuring a clear understanding of responsibilities.
- Board members should avoid stepping into operational matters, while executives should respect the board's governance function.

### Constructive conflict and resolution

- Disagreements should be encouraged as part of healthy governance.

- Boards and executives should engage in discussions with a problem-solving mindset rather than an adversarial approach.
- Conflict resolution mechanisms should be in place to manage disputes effectively.

**Evaluation and continuous improvement**

- Regular board and executive performance assessments help in identifying areas for improvement.
- Boards should evaluate their own effectiveness as well as the CEO's performance.
- A structured feedback mechanism should be established to refine governance processes.

## Best Practices for Effective Collaboration

**Regular and meaningful engagement**

- Scheduled board meetings should focus on substantive discussions rather than routine updates.
- Additional off-cycle meetings, retreats, and informal discussions can strengthen the working relationship.

- Executives should proactively engage board members outside of formal meetings.

### Utilizing board expertise

- Board members are often industry veterans with valuable insights and expertise.
- CEOs should leverage the board's expertise for guidance on strategic decisions, mergers and acquisitions, and industry trends.
- Board members should be involved in mentorship roles for key executives.

### CEO and board chair collaboration

- A strong relationship between the CEO and the board chair sets the tone for overall board engagement.
- Regular one-on-one discussions help align priorities and ensure smooth governance.

### Crisis management and board involvement

- In times of crisis, such as financial downturns or reputational risks, boards should be actively engaged.

- Clear crisis protocols should be established to ensure rapid and coordinated responses.

**Succession planning**

- A collaborative approach to CEO and executive succession planning ensures continuity of leadership.
- The board should work closely with the CEO to identify and groom future leaders.

## Case Studies: CEOs with Strong Board Relationships

***Jay Malave, L3Harris Technologies***

L3Harris Technologies, a mid-cap aerospace and defense firm, has demonstrated strong board-executive collaboration under the leadership of CFO Jay Malave. Malave played a key role in ensuring transparency in financial reporting and strategic decision-making. His ability to communicate effectively with the board strengthened investor confidence and strategic execution.

***Laura Alber, Williams-Sonoma***

Laura Alber, CEO of Williams-Sonoma, built a strong relationship with her board, leading to impressive financial growth and strategic expansion. Under her leadership, the company effectively navigated e-commerce disruptions and supply chain challenges. Her ability to engage the board in strategic discussions and decision-making contributed to the company's resilience and success.

## Conclusion

An effective relationship between the C-suite and the Board of Directors is essential for corporate success. By fostering transparency, trust, strategic alignment, and active collaboration, companies can ensure strong governance and sustainable growth. Executives who prioritize board engagement, such as Jay Malave and Laura Alber, exemplify the benefits of a well-functioning executive-board relationship. Companies that invest in strengthening these dynamics position themselves for long-term success in an increasingly complex business environment.

# Section III: Play Politics Without Selling Your Soul

## You Must Understand the Rules

In any organization, political savvy is a critical skill for leaders at all levels. The ability to navigate internal dynamics, influence stakeholders, and build strategic relationships can mean the difference between success and stagnation. Political savvy is especially crucial for the C-suite, where executives must align diverse interests, manage conflicts, and drive the company's vision forward.

## Understanding Political Savvy in an Organization

Political savvy refers to the ability to read the organizational landscape, understand power dynamics, and influence key players to achieve desired outcomes. It is not about manipulation but rather about strategic engagement, diplomacy, and relationship-building. Leaders who exhibit political savvy are adept at:

- **Building Networks:** They cultivate relationships across the organization to gain insights, garner support, and drive initiatives.

- **Understanding Power Structures:** They recognize formal and informal power centers and navigate them effectively.

- **Communicating Persuasively:** They tailor their messaging to different stakeholders to ensure alignment and buy-in.

- **Managing Conflict:** They address disagreements constructively and seek solutions that serve the organization's best interests.

- **Driving Change:** They leverage their influence to implement new strategies and foster innovation.

## The Role of the C-Suite in Political Relationship Management

The C-suite plays a crucial role in managing political relationships within an organization. Their responsibilities in this regard include:

**Aligning Stakeholders With the Company's Vision:** C-suite leaders must ensure that all stakeholders—employees, board members, investors, and partners—are aligned with the company's strategic direction. This requires skillful negotiation and persuasion to create a shared understanding and commitment.

**Managing Board and Investor Relations:** Executives, particularly the CEO and CFO, must navigate boardroom politics and maintain investor confidence. Political savvy helps them present financial performance, strategic initiatives, and market positioning in a way that satisfies shareholders while ensuring long-term growth.

**Influencing Corporate Culture:** Corporate culture is shaped at the top. Politically savvy C-suite leaders set the tone for collaboration, transparency, and ethical decision-making. They must balance competing interests while fostering a culture of trust and accountability.

**Leading Through Change and Crisis:** Whether managing a merger, restructuring, or industry disruption, the C-suite must guide the organization through change. Political acumen helps them anticipate resistance, address concerns, and secure buy-in from key players.

**Navigating Internal Power Dynamics:** Organizations have power structures that are both formal (hierarchical) and informal (influence-based). Executives must identify key influencers and decision-makers to ensure smooth operations and avoid political missteps.

## Case Studies: CEOs Who Exhibit Political Savvy

### ***Satya Nadella, Microsoft***

Although Microsoft is now a large-cap company, its transformation under Satya Nadella highlights how political savvy can reshape an organization. Nadella inherited a company with internal divisions, a combative culture, and a stagnating innovation pipeline. His ability to unite warring factions, shift the corporate culture toward collaboration, and gain board and investor confidence played a significant role in Microsoft's resurgence.

Nadella used political savvy to:

- reframe Microsoft's mission around a growth mindset and cloud computing.
- foster partnerships with competitors like Linux and open-source communities.
- align employees, leadership, and investors on long-term strategic objectives.

***Marillyn Hewson, Lockheed Martin***

Marillyn Hewson, former CEO of Lockheed Martin, demonstrated exceptional political savvy in managing government relations, internal stakeholder alignment, and organizational strategy. Under her leadership, Lockheed Martin secured significant defense contracts and strengthened its market position.

Hewson's political savvy was evident in the way she:

- effectively navigated government and regulatory relationships to win major contracts.
- aligned internal leadership on critical business decisions.
- managed high-stakes negotiations and mergers, including Lockheed's acquisition of Sikorsky Aircraft.

## Conclusion

Political savvy is an indispensable skill for leaders at all levels, particularly in the C-suite. Smaller and mid-cap companies, in particular, benefit from executives who can strategically navigate power dynamics, build consensus, and drive the organization forward. By fostering relationships, aligning stakeholders, and leveraging influence, politically astute executives ensure the long-term success and stability of their organizations. CEOs like Satya Nadella and Marillyn Hewson exemplify how political acumen can transform businesses, making political savvy an essential competency for all executives aiming to lead effectively in complex organizational landscapes.

## Section IV: Lead Across Borders and Cultures

### Global Teams Need Global-Minded Leaders

Organizations must continuously adapt to market dynamics, technological advancements, and shifting customer expectations. Companies seeking to remain competitive, drive innovation, and ensure long-term sustainability must negotiate change and transformation with grace. However, managing organizational change is complex and requires strong leadership from the C-suite.

The role of C-suite executives in change management extends beyond decision-making; they must function as visionaries, communicators, strategists, and role models. Successful change initiatives demand sharp vision, well-defined strategies, stakeholder engagement, and a disciplined execution plan. Without strong leadership from the top, transformation efforts risk failure due to resistance, misalignment, or lack of execution.

### The C-Suite's Role in Leading Change and Transformation

Change management is the structured approach of transitioning individuals, teams, and organizations from a current state to a desired future state. Transformation, on the other hand, represents a more profound and strategic shift that often redefines business models, company culture, or operations.

The C-suite plays a pivotal role in ensuring that change initiatives are aligned with the company's mission, values, and long-term goals. Below are the key ways the C-suite leads an organization through change.

**Establishing a clear vision for change**

The foundation of any successful transformation is a clear and compelling vision. The CEO and C-suite must define what the change entails, why it is necessary, and how it aligns with the company's broader goals.

- **Why Vision Matters:** Without a well-articulated vision, employees may struggle to understand the purpose of change and resist it.

- **Defining a Vision:** A compelling vision should inspire employees, customers, and stakeholders while providing a road map for execution.

**Example:** When Anne Mulcahy became CEO of Xerox in 2001, the company was on the brink of bankruptcy, with billions in debt. Without a background in finance, she made the tough decision to cut costs, refocus on Xerox's core business, and invest in innovation. By rebuilding trust with employees and stakeholders, she successfully led one of the most respected corporate turnarounds of the early 2000s.

### Communicating the change effectively

Clear and transparent communication is essential for successful change management. Employees need to understand what is changing, why, and how it will impact their roles. The C-suite must lead these conversations with authenticity and empathy.

Best practices in communication:

- Regularly update employees through town halls, newsletters, and team meetings.
- Address employee concerns and provide a platform for them to share feedback.
- Use data-driven insights to reinforce the need for change.

**Example:** When Reed Hastings led Netflix through its transition from DVD rentals to streaming, he made a bold bet on the future of digital content. Despite initial backlash, including a stock drop and subscriber loss, Hastings stayed the course. His long-term vision transformed Netflix into a global entertainment powerhouse and redefined how the world consumes media.

### Creating a culture that embraces change

Company culture can be a major barrier or a catalyst for transformation. If employees are accustomed to stability, resistance to change can be high. The C-suite must embed adaptability, resilience, and innovation into the company culture. In a change-ready culture:

- a mindset of continuous improvement is fostered.
- employees are rewarded for embracing and driving change.
- open dialogue and feedback are encouraged.

**Example:** When Rosalind Brewer took the helm as CEO of Walgreens Boots Alliance, she prioritized digital transformation and health equity amid the COVID-19 pandemic. She expanded the company's vaccination efforts, strengthened partnerships with health-care providers, and invested in technology to modernize the customer experience. Brewer's leadership positioned Walgreens as a more agile, health-focused organization ready to meet the evolving needs of consumers.

### Engaging and empowering employees

Change initiatives succeed when employees feel they are part of the transformation rather than victims of it. C-suite leaders should engage employees at all levels, providing them with opportunities to contribute and take ownership of change. Some tactics to improve employee engagement include:

- Involve employees in decision-making processes.
- Offer training and development to help employees adapt.

- Recognize and reward employees who champion change.

**Example:** When Marvin Ellison became CEO of Lowe's, he focused on operational efficiency and empowering store employees to better serve customers. He streamlined inventory management, invested in employee training, and modernized technology systems. These changes improved customer satisfaction and helped Lowe's strengthen its position in the highly competitive home improvement market.

### Aligning organizational structure and processes

To sustain transformation, companies often need to realign their structures, processes, and technology to ensure ongoing effectiveness. The C-suite must ensure that internal systems support the change initiative. The following steps can help align an organization:

- Evaluate whether the current leadership structure supports transformation.
- Remove outdated processes that hinder agility.
- Invest in technology and innovation.

**Example:** At Starbucks, CEO Howard Schultz led a dramatic turnaround during the 2008 financial crisis. He refocused the company on its core values, closed underperforming stores, and invested heavily in employee training and customer experience. Schultz also championed the introduction of mobile ordering and digital payments, helping Starbucks evolve into a tech-enabled brand while preserving its human-centered culture. His leadership blended strategic reinvention with operational discipline, reigniting growth and customer loyalty.

## Managing resistance to change

Resistance to change is natural, especially in long-established organizations. C-suite executives must identify sources of resistance and proactively address them.

Some common barriers to change include:

- fear of job loss or skill redundancy.
- skepticism about leadership's motives.
- comfort with the status quo.

Resistance can be overcome with strategies such as:

- providing clear explanations of benefits.
- offering retraining and career development.
- leading by example; executives must embrace change before expecting employees to do so.

**Example:** When Ford transitioned to electric vehicles, leadership had to address resistance from traditional auto workers. The company provided retraining programs to ease the transition.

## Case Studies: CEOs Who Led Successful Change

***Brian Niccol, Chipotle Mexican Grill***

Before Brian Niccol's arrival as CEO, Chipotle, a mid-cap fast-casual restaurant chain specializing in Mexican cuisine, struggled with food safety concerns, declining sales, and an outdated business model.

Transformation strategy:

- Niccol prioritized digital transformation, launching mobile ordering and delivery services.
- He focused on brand repositioning, re-establishing trust in Chipotle's commitment to fresh ingredients.
- Operational improvements led to better customer experiences and faster service times.

Results:

- Digital sales grew exponentially, contributing to Chipotle's revenue growth.
- Customer confidence returned, resulting in more foot traffic.
- Stock value increased, positioning Chipotle for long-term success.

***Patrick Doyle, Domino's Pizza***

Domino's was once seen as a struggling pizza chain with subpar food quality and outdated ordering systems. Patrick Doyle, who served as CEO from 2010 to 2018, led a bold transformation.

Transformation strategy:

- Doyle invested in online ordering, mobile apps, and AI-powered delivery tracking.
- He acknowledged past failures and rebranded the company as a customer-first, innovation-driven brand.
- New store designs optimized delivery speed, which improved customer satisfaction.

Results:

- Domino's became the world's top pizza delivery brand.
- Sales surged, and the chain's market share grew substantially.
- The company set the standard for digital transformation in the food industry.

## Conclusion

Leading an organization through change and transformation is one of the most challenging yet most essential responsibilities of the C-suite. Without strong leadership, change initiatives risk failure due to misalignment, resistance, and lack of execution.

The most effective C-suite leaders:

- establish a clear vision and communicate it effectively.
- build a culture that embraces change and innovation.
- engage employees and empower them to contribute to transformation.
- align organizational structure, technology, and processes with change objectives.
- manage resistance through transparency and support.

CEOs like Brian Niccol and Patrick Doyle demonstrate how strategic transformation can reposition a company for long-term success. Their leadership in digital adoption, operational efficiency, and cultural change turned struggling brands into market leaders.

For businesses navigating change, the lesson is clear: Transformation must be led from the top, with a clear strategy, effective communication, and an unwavering commitment to execution.

# 8

# Conversations From the C-Suite

## Tammy Jersey: 5 Critical Skills for the Future-Proof CEO

Tammy Jersey never intended to build a leadership empire—she just couldn't stand watching executives burn out, bottom out, or check out. After two decades of executive coaching, organizational transformation, and talent strategy, she'd seen one thing over and over again: brilliant leaders undone by blind spots, bloated egos, or bureaucratic inertia.

Now, as CEO and founder of TKJ Leadership, Tammy sits at the intersection of business growth and human potential. Her firm partners with boards, CEOs, and executive teams to help develop leaders who can endure, evolve, and inspire, even when the winds of business threaten to blow them off course.

Tammy's clients range from high-growth startups to private equity-backed companies and mature enterprises. Across industries, boardrooms, and balance sheets, one question echoes louder than the rest: "What skills will define the next great CEO?"

Tammy answers the question with conviction born of experience:

"The best CEOs in the next five years won't just be smarter or faster—they'll be more human, more adaptable, and more strategically intentional than ever before."

As a leadership coach and mentor, Tammy has identified the Top 5 Critical Skills Every CEO Must Master to thrive in an increasingly complex, volatile, and values-driven world.

## Strategic Curiosity: Ask Bold Questions

"The most dangerous leaders I coach are the ones who think they've already figured it out."

CEOs are expected to have *answers*, but the most successful ones are driven by *questions*. Strategic curiosity, Tammy explains, isn't about wandering—it's about wondering with purpose.

With developments in AI, global supply chains, climate risk, and stakeholder capitalism driving the business landscape, static thinking will be the death of innovation. Tammy tells the story of a CEO in a tech company who—despite being a former engineer—spent 90% of the executives' strategic time asking nontechnical questions:

- "What do our customers need that they don't know how to ask for?"
- "What's the one assumption we've never challenged?"
- "If we started from scratch, how would we build this company differently?"

That CEO tripled revenue in 24 months. Why? Because curiosity created breakthroughs, not just marginal gains.

**Tammy's Takeaway:**

Curiosity isn't a luxury. It's a leadership muscle. CEOs must model it openly and institutionalize it relentlessly.

## Leadership Agility: Lead Through Uncertainty, Not Around It

The pandemic proved what Tammy has always believed: Every CEO is a crisis leader.

But agility is not just about reacting faster—it's about knowing when to pivot, when to persist, and how to calibrate teams along the way. Tammy describes agility as an "emotional GPS"—the ability to navigate shifting priorities while maintaining direction and culture.

She shares the story of a manufacturing CEO who resisted layoffs during COVID by redeploying workers into temporary roles, retraining them with micro-learning tools, and redesigning workflow to boost productivity. Instead of panicking, that CEO adapted with intention.

Agility, Tammy argues, is a blend of data fluency, emotional intelligence, and operational intuition. It's knowing when to move, but also how to bring your people with you.

**Tammy's Takeaway:**

Agility isn't just speed. It's synchronized movement with your business, your people, and your values—especially when the ground beneath you shifts.

## Stakeholder Empathy: Build Trust by Listening Harder

Tammy doesn't mince words:

"If you can't feel what your employees, customers, investors, and community care about, you won't be a CEO for long."

She believes empathy is now a competitive advantage.

Today's CEOs are leading in an era of polarization, generational shifts, and social scrutiny. In this new environment, empathy isn't about hand-holding—it's about strategic listening. Tammy points to a health-care CEO who tripled employee engagement by spending the first 15 minutes of every executive meeting reviewing anonymous staff pulse survey comments. Not metrics—*voices*.

What emerged wasn't just better morale. It was better decision-making.

CEOs who understand stakeholders' fears, motivations, and values can anticipate issues before they erupt—and build loyalty that outlasts quarterly earnings.

**Tammy's Takeaway:**

Empathy without strategy is soft. Strategy without empathy is brittle. The next-generation CEO must bring both to the table to build a business that is flexible enough to bend and strong enough to thrive.

## Narrative Authority: Shape the Story Before Someone Else Does

Tammy knows from experience: Narrative beats numbers. CEOs who lead without a compelling story leave a vacuum that others will fill—investors, employees, media, or competitors.

As attention spans shrink and information floods inboxes, narrative authority is how CEOs anchor *why* the company exists, *where* it's headed, and *what* the path forward means.

She recalls a retail CEO navigating a painful restructuring. Instead of hiding behind consultants, he took the mic at town halls and told the story himself:

- why the industry was changing
- what values were guiding the decisions
- how they would support people through the shift

The result? Record-low attrition during downsizing and an uptick in Glassdoor ratings.

**Tammy's Takeaway:**

CEOs must learn to wield narrative not as spin, but as a strategic tool for alignment. Storytelling isn't just marketing—it's mission-critical.

## Culture Execution: Operationalize the "How," Not Just the "What"

Culture used to be an HR buzzword. Now it's a board-level issue—and CEOs must own it.

Tammy believes the best CEOs are cultural architects. They embed values into daily behaviors, hiring practices, and decision criteria. But here's her twist: It's not enough to inspire culture. You must execute it.

Tammy shares a case study of a logistics CEO who hardwired the company's "Speed with Purpose" value into operations. Key performance indicators (KPIs), bonus structures, and customer feedback loops were all re-engineered to reflect the company's values. Culture wasn't a poster on the wall—it was a process in motion.

The company saw a 40% reduction in turnover and landed two new Fortune 500 clients.

**Tammy's Takeaway:**

If you can't measure your culture, you can't manage it. And if you can't manage it, you can't scale it.

## CEOs of the Future Are Systems Thinkers With Soul

As our conversation winds down, Tammy leans back and smiles. "Let's be honest," she says, "the CEO myth is still alive—the idea that one person can have all the answers, never show doubt, and drive results like a machine."

But the CEOs who will *thrive* in the coming years won't be superheroes.

"They'll be human-centered systems thinkers—people who can see the whole, empower the parts, and communicate the why."

Tammy closes with one last insight:

"Being a great CEO isn't about being the smartest person in the room. It's about building a room full of smart people who trust your leadership enough to follow you into the unknown."

That trust is earned not by perfection, but by presence.

It's sustained not by power, but by purpose.

And it's scaled not by control, but by clarity.

## Final Word: Tammy Jersey's 5 to Thrive

1. **Strategic Curiosity**: Replace certainty with inquiry.

2. **Leadership Agility**: Pivot with purpose, not panic.

3. **Stakeholder Empathy**: Listen like a leader, not a lifeguard.

4. **Narrative Authority**: Own the story or be owned by it.

5. **Culture Execution**: Build culture into operations.

These are not "soft" skills. They are scalable, strategic, and sustainable.

They are the difference between CEOs who *manage* and those who *lead*.

And they are the foundation upon which the next era of C-suite success will be built.

## Erica Jain: Leading with Purpose, Building for Impact

Erica Jain did not follow the traditional MBA-to-corporate executive playbook. After completing her undergraduate degree at Duke University and enrolling at Wharton, she made the unconventional decision to step away from her MBA in the mid-2010s. Alongside co-founder Cavan Klinsky, Erica built Healthie with a mission to take on one of the country's biggest sore spots: the U.S. health-care system.

From the start, Erica and Cavan shared a vision for delivering patient-centric, longitudinal care through a scalable platform that did not just manage health care but actively improved it. Based in Midtown Manhattan, Erica leads Healthie with calm intensity and unwavering focus, while Cavan brings a relentless drive to build the technology that powers this transformation. Together, they are driven not by valuations or headlines but by a deep curiosity and a belief that health-care delivery in America needs a systemic overhaul.

### Built to Last, Not Just to Sell

Erica leads with a "marathon over sprint" mindset. She is building for durability—not for short-term spikes or quick exits. At Healthie, success is measured in customer outcomes and long-term trust, not in flashy fundraising announcements.

Healthie's culture and decision-making are grounded in three guiding values:

- **Respect:** For users, teammates, and the mission

- **Resilience:** Staying focused and adaptive through market shifts

- **Reliability:** In health care, trust is foundational

While many founders chase visibility, Erica remains laser-focused on delivering meaningful results for both patients and providers.

## Solving What's Broken in Health Care

With a focus on electronic health records (EHRs) and practice management, Healthie tackles some of the deepest flaws in health-care delivery:

- **Fragmented, Episodic Care:** Traditional models revolve around brief, infrequent visits. Healthie enables continuous engagement and care.

- **Siloed Providers:** Health-care teams often work in isolation. Healthie brings them together with shared tools and insights.

- **Manual, Outdated Workflows:** Healthie automates paper-based and time-consuming scheduling, charting, and billing.

- **Poor User Experience:** Most EHRs frustrate clinicians. Healthie earns unusually high NPS scores with its patient- and provider-friendly design.

- **Disjointed Coordination:** Healthie ensures providers can "close the loop" in care transitions with seamless referrals and communication.

## The Platform: Modern Care, Powered by Tech

Healthie's platform is built to support both longitudinal care and collaborative care, empowering providers to work together and stay connected with patients over time.

### Longitudinal Care Features

- **Relationship-Based Architecture:** Designed to support long-term patient-provider connections.

- **Ongoing Communication:** Secure messaging, virtual check-ins, and follow-up tools.

- **Custom Workflows:** Supports chronic care, integrative health, and virtual-first models.

- **Patient-Centric UI:** A rare EHR that focuses on the care journey, not just documentation.

**Collaborative Care Features**

- **Multi-Provider Access:** Shared patient records across care teams.

- **Team-Based Planning:** Unified notes, schedules, and messaging.

- **Integrated Operations:** Merging clinical and administrative workflows for full visibility.

This dual focus positions Healthie as the operating system for modern health-care teams delivering whole-person care.

## Customer Support: The Engine for Innovation

At Healthie, customer satisfaction is not a department, it is a strategy. Erica personally monitors feedback and support tickets. Her philosophy is, "Customer support is product development."

Key principles include:

- **Founder Involvement:** Erica stays directly connected to customer voices through weekly check-ins that set the stage for quick course corrections.

- **Over-Investment in Support:** Resources outpace industry norms—by design.

- **Weekly Feedback Loops:** Customer support insights go

straight into product discussions.

- **High-Stakes Reliability:** In health care, downtime is a risk to patient safety. Trust is nonnegotiable.

The result? Ninety percent of Healthie's growth is referral-driven—proof that the product and support experience speak for themselves.

## Strategic, Not Splashy: Product Mapping Done Right

Healthie's product road map follows a simple yet powerful ethos: "If you say something, do something."

Instead of chasing trends or shiny features, the team builds with discipline:

- **Customer Insight:** Product needs surface through real frontline feedback.
- **Multi-Year Vision:** Every release considers long-term care evolution.
- **Industry Responsiveness:** From virtual care to remote monitoring, Healthie adapts early.
- **Operational Scale:** Manual processes become scalable systems over time.

With $42 million raised—and profitability achieved for much of its journey—Healthie remains free from short-term investor pressure. Every decision is made with the user, not the optics, in mind.

## Leadership that Listens, Culture that Performs

Erica leads with presence, not pretense. Her style is calm, collaborative, and intensely mission driven. Healthie's entire team reflects that tone—low ego, high accountability, and relentless curiosity.

Erica and Cavan built a company where culture is more than lip service; it is the operating system. Employees are not just told what matters; they live it through shared values and clear expectations.

In our conversation, Erica even offered to help share this book with the Wharton community—a testament to her generosity and commitment to lifting others up.

## Rebuilding Health Care, One Relationship at a Time

What makes Erica stand out as a C-suite leader is not just her operational excellence or industry insight. It is her belief that leadership is a service and that building something meaningful requires clarity, consistency, and care.

She is not managing her way to success. She is leading—with purpose, discipline, and humanity.

This is exactly the kind of leadership this book celebrates and promotes.

## Jessica Klodnicki: Building Bold Cultures and Agile Teams

When I sat down with Jessica Klodnicki, former CEO of KT Tape and seasoned executive in the consumer products and outdoor lifestyle industries, it quickly became clear why she is a standout C-suite leader. With a career spanning product development, brand transformation, global general management, and private equity-backed business turnarounds, Jessica brings a rare combination of marketing savvy, operational grit, and cultural fluency to every organization she touches.

In our conversation, Jessica unpacked the experiences and philosophies that have shaped her leadership journey—from an entrepreneurial start in product development to running global brands and revitalizing tired cultures into energized, mission-driven teams.

### From Product Manager to C-Suite Trailblazer

Jessica's path to the top began in an unexpected way: Right out of undergrad, she found herself in product development at a small, family-run baby products company. "There were no silos," she recalls. "I had to figure it all out—sourcing, marketing, design, operations. It was a crash course in general management."

By 24, she was leading all of marketing and product development—rare responsibilities for anyone so early in their career. That direct experience gave her a taste for entrepreneurial energy, but she recognized the need to complement it with structure. That is when she joined Newell Brands, where she learned the discipline and operating rhythm of a global public company— "regular checkpoints, business reviews, cross-functional planning. It was not about bureaucracy. It was about building alignment and speed." Jessica ran marketing and product for several business units, even completing an expat assignment in Paris, which challenged her to lead across cultures.

"I was one of only two Americans on a truly global team. It was not just corporate culture—it was national cultures," Jessica says. "That experience helped me develop the adaptability and situational awareness that's served me ever since."

## A Passion for Sports, Outdoors, and Purpose

As a lifelong athlete, marathoner, triathlete, and golfer, Jessica always dreamt of aligning her passions with her profession. She eventually did so in roles at Mizuno and later with Bell helmets at Easton Bell Sports, where she took on her first official general manager role. She relished the opportunity to combine a love for outdoor adventure with sharp business execution.

"Bell was a $200 million portfolio," she explains. "It was my first time working with private equity, and the goal was clear—prepare the business for a sale."

Jessica led a full transformation: reigniting innovation, refreshing the brand, driving growth, and implementing a disciplined operating rhythm. That effort resulted in a successful sale to Vista Outdoor and led her to take on leadership of Camelbak and other brands.

The experience also taught her something important: "I love the private equity environment. There's clarity of mission, a defined timeline, and the freedom to make smart decisions without the noise of quarterly earnings pressure," she says.

## Turning Around Culture and Performance at KT

In 2022, Jessica took on her first official CEO role when she became head of KT Tape, an elastic sports tape designed to provide support and pain relief to muscles, joints, and ligaments. What she walked into was a brand with enormous consumer love but an internal culture that had lost its spark.

"On day one, it was gray—literally and emotionally," she shares. "Tall cubicles, silence, no energy. Then I would go to events and see people freaking out about our brand. The disconnect was jarring."

Jessica launched an employee engagement survey on day two. The NPS score was 17. "That's how we knew the work ahead wasn't just business strategy—it was cultural transformation."

Under her leadership, KT underwent a full brand and cultural relaunch. Vision and values were defined from within—not by an outside agency. Transparency became a pillar. Jessica put every employee, from warehouse to C-suite, on the same bonus structure. Monthly all-hands meetings shared strategy and performance in plain language. The employee NPS soared to 64 by the time she left, and the company completed a successful transaction in under three years.

"It wasn't rocket science," she said. "It was getting back to fundamentals—clarity, communication, connection."

## Leadership Skills That Matter in the Modern C-Suite

Jessica credits her success to three central leadership capabilities:

1. **Situational Leadership:** "You have to be the chameleon," she says. "Flex to the needs of your team. Some leaders try to bend others to fit their style. That is a mistake. Great leaders adapt."

2. **Simplification and Clarity:** Whether at KT or Bell or Skullcandy, Jessica's leadership shows her belief in distilling complex strategies into a few clear growth levers. "Everyone from the CFO to the warehouse team should be able to name our top five priorities. That is how you enable smart, decentralized decision-making."

3. **Radical Candor:** A mentor at Newell taught Jessica the power of direct, compassionate feedback. "I didn't have the words for it then, but now I call it 'radical candor,'" she says, referring to the concept popularized by best-selling author and feedback trainer Kim Scott. "When people know the feedback comes from a place of support, they embrace it. That built trust across my teams."

## A Vision for Leadership in the Coming Years

When asked what C-suite leaders will need most in the years ahead, Jessica offers a concise but powerful road map:

- **Speed and Agility:** "Leaders need to know when to change the line without changing the destination," she says, alluding to her love for mountain biking.

- **Decentralized Leadership:** "People closest to the work should be empowered to act. That only works if the mission is clear."

- **Clear Operating Rhythm:** "Discipline equals freedom," she says, quoting leadership expert Jocko Willink. "It is not about bureaucracy. It is about creating structure so teams can move fast and smart."

- **Trust and Transparency:** "Culture is not fluff. It is a performance driver. I have seen quiet, gray buildings come alive—and it impacts everything."

- **Purpose-Driven Engagement:** "We did quarterly wellness outings at KT—pickleball, curling, even a couch-to-5k. Some people outside the organization might have perceived these types of activities as frivolous. But when people compete together, sweat together, they collaborate better. Culture is the strategy."

Jessica's track record includes brand reinvention, cultural turnaround, and commercial acceleration at both entrepreneurial startups and global corporations. From Newell Brands to Bell Helmets, Mizuno, Skullcandy, and KT, she has worn the hats of general manager, CMO, and CEO, all with a consistent throughline: Lead with purpose, act with clarity, and build cultures that thrive.

But what really sets Jessica apart is her ability to distill leadership to its core elements—simplicity, trust, empowerment, and honest communication. Her story is a blueprint for every executive who wants to stop managing and start leading.

## Simplicity: A Leadership Superpower

In today's complexity-heavy world, Jessica is a firm believer in the power of simplicity.

"Complex strategies do not move people—clear ones do. My job as a leader is to make the complex understandable, actionable, and energizing."

At KT and previous roles, she distilled strategy into five key priorities that every team member—from CFO to warehouse associate—could name. "If people do not understand what success looks like, they cannot own it. Simplicity is how you scale."

This clarity enabled faster decision-making and decentralized leadership, a model she champions strongly.

## Decentralized Leadership and Staying on Mission

Jessica believes that the only way to move fast and scale responsibly is by pushing decision-making closer to the action. "When people know the strategy, they don't need to wait for permission," she explains.

Drawing inspiration from Willink's book *Extreme Ownership* (St. Martin's Press), she adopted the principle of decentralized leadership, aligning teams around a mission and trusting them to execute.

At KT, that meant cross-functional teams had the autonomy to act, innovate, and solve problems independently—without endless escalation. "Agility does not happen from the top down. It happens when the front lines know what to do and feel trusted to do it."

## Culture as a Catalyst

When Jessica joined KT as CEO, the brand was loved by customers but lacked internal energy. "It was quiet—literally gray," she says. "People came in, did their job, and left. But the brand was about energy, movement, recovery. That needed to be reflected inside, too."

Within days, she launched a cultural reboot. The team crafted a new vision and set of values *together*—no external agency required. She unified the company with one bonus structure, monthly huddles, transparent financial reporting, and company-wide wellness events.

"Culture is not a slide deck—it is a shared experience. And when people feel safe, seen, and connected, everything gets better," she says.

## Situational Leadership and Team Flexibility

A core philosophy Jessica has embraced throughout her career is situational leadership—meeting people where they are, not where you want them to be.

"No two employees need the same thing. As a leader, I don't expect others to flex to me. I flex to them," she says.

This mindset was shaped by her early exposure to different work cultures—including her expat assignment in Paris and time with Japanese-owned Mizuno. "Being a military brat growing up also helped," she says. "I learned to drop into new environments, listen, adjust, and find connection."

She credits much of her leadership success to this chameleon-like adaptability, especially when managing cross-functional teams with diverse personalities and skill sets.

## Radical Candor and the Power of Honest Feedback

Another leadership lesson that shaped Jessica's approach came from a mentor at Newell who modeled direct, constructive feedback.

"He was tough, but you knew he cared. His honesty was not about control—it was about growth," she says.

Later, she found the perfect words for this approach in Scott's book *Radical Candor* (St. Martin's Press. "It validated what I felt: When people know you care, they will listen to hard truths. And they will grow from it," Jessica says.

Jessica now builds this feedback culture into every company she leads, creating psychological safety, promoting transparent dialogue, and eliminating fear of failure. "Open, respectful communication drives innovation. It is how teams learn, iterate, and win."

## Speed, Agility, and Disciplined Execution

Today's business environment demands rapid response, strategic pivots, and an ability to execute under pressure. For Jessica, speed and agility are nonnegotiable.

"The terrain is always changing," she says. "Think of it like mountain biking, you know the destination, but the trail shifts. You have to find the line that works and adjust in real time."

This agility is only possible with a disciplined foundation. She reinforces operating cadence, goal alignment, and strategic focus—not as constraints, but as enablers.

"Discipline equals freedom. It gives you room to move without chaos. That is especially important in smaller, high-growth businesses."

## A Leader for the Modern C-Suite

As we conclude our conversation, I ask Jessica what she believes the next generation of C-suite leaders must develop to thrive. She does not hesitate:

- **Simplicity in Strategy:** "Make the path clear. If it is not simple, it will not scale."
- **Situational Leadership:** "One style does not fit all. Learn to flex to your team."
- **Direct, Honest Feedback:** "Radical candor creates trust. Trust builds performance."
- **Decentralized Decision-Making:** "Push ownership to the front lines."
- **Cultural Accountability:** "Your values should shape behavior, not sit in a binder."
- **Speed and Agility with Discipline:** "Be fast—but with purpose."

Her parting words are as clear as her leadership philosophy:

"Leadership is not about control. It is about clarity, compassion, and conviction. People want to be seen, trusted, and empowered. If you can give them that—while staying focused on your mission—you will build teams that can do anything."

## Final Reflections

Jessica's career spans both corporate titans and scrappy innovators, from Paris to Park City. Through it all, she has been guided by adaptability, authenticity, and an unwavering belief in the power of culture to drive business outcomes.

As we wrap, she offers one last piece of advice: "If you are uncomfortable with culture, get comfortable. It is not soft—it is the glue."

With a track record of transforming brands, energizing teams, and scaling performance under pressure, Jessica exemplifies what *Start Leading, Stop Managing* is all about.

Jessica Klodnicki's story is more than a career profile—it is a lesson in how to lead with vision and humanity. She does not just lead companies through transformations, she leads people toward belief in themselves, belief in each other, and belief in the mission.

## Maria Warrington: From Uncertain Beginnings to CEO

Maria Warrington's professional journey did not start with a plan to lead a company. As a sophomore at Tufts University, she was at a crossroads, shifting away from a pre-med track that suddenly felt overwhelming. "I was always such a good student," Warrington recalls. "But when I got to college, I just wanted to have a little fun." That moment of release turned into a pivotal redirection.

Inspired by friends in business programs at Bentley University and Babson College, she changed her major to economics. Though Tufts lacked a formal business curriculum, economics opened a pathway into the business world—and soon, into a career that would span finance, operations, and executive leadership in iconic consumer brands.

### Launching a Career in Retail and Consumer Brands

After college internships in finance left her uninspired, a senior-year accounting course unexpectedly clicked. "It came naturally to me," she says. That realization led her to a specialized master's program in accounting and business at Northeastern University, where she joined PricewaterhouseCoopers (PwC) through a cooperative education experience.

Maria's first audit assignment was with Stride Rite, a household name in children's footwear. It was the beginning of a 13-year trajectory that would see her grow from consultant to senior director. At Stride Rite, she found her first professional mentor, a female VP who embodied the career Warrington aspired to build. "That was it," she says. "That was the job I wanted."

Over the next several years, she moved internally from PwC to Stride Rite, leveraging relationships and volunteer projects to gain visibility. Her career married personal interest—fashion, retail, beauty—with professional strength in finance and operations. Her north star was clear, and she took deliberate steps to follow it.

## Climbing the Ladder at Wolverine Worldwide

When Stride Rite was acquired by Wolverine Worldwide, Warrington continued to thrive. She progressed from Keds to Sperry and ultimately led the Boston Group, overseeing finance and operations across four brands: Saucony, Sperry, Keds, and Stride Rite. As responsibilities grew, so did her team. Eventually she managed more than 40 people across e-commerce, financial planning, merchandising, and technical functions.

"I had strong mentors," she explains. "And I made sure to build real relationships across functions—not just being the finance 'stop sign,' but working alongside marketing, sales, and product to solve problems together."

Her approach: Be a strategic partner, not a gatekeeper.

## Motherhood, Confidence, and Career Rebalancing

Maria's path was not without its personal challenges. When she became a mother at 30, she questioned whether she could juggle career and parenthood. "I just remember thinking, I can't do both," she says. But after navigating the chaos of early parenthood—daycare illnesses, doctor visits, sleep deprivation—she emerged with renewed confidence.

"Having kids changed how I showed up at work," Warrington says. "I stressed less about what people thought. I became more vocal, more confident, and less afraid to speak up."

That personal growth ignited her professional development. Formerly quiet and introverted—"a blue-red on the color wheel," she remembers—she started to lean into leadership more fully, letting her voice and perspective shape outcomes in the room.

## Exposure to Women's Brands and a New Calling

During her time at Keds, Warrington worked on an all-female leadership team. The brand's heritage—originally created for women in the early 1900s—carried a mission of empowerment. That exposure to female-driven messaging, health, and beauty brands sparked a new interest.

As she approached her 40s, that interest became more personal. When a recruiter introduced her to Beacon Wellness Brands, a private equity-backed business in the women's health and sexual wellness space, it felt unfamiliar—but intriguing. "The term 'sexual wellness' meant nothing to me at the time," she admits. But the more she learned, the more she connected.

## A New Chapter: CFO to CEO

Warrington joined Beacon Wellness as CFO, brought in to professionalize a high-revenue startup still operating like a small business. She quickly implemented systems, introduced financial rigor, and helped manage tensions between the founder, the private equity firm, and the evolving leadership team.

Within two years—and after three different CEOs—Warrington was promoted to CEO herself.

"In the big CPG [consumer packaged goods] world I came from, CEOs usually came from marketing or sales," she notes. "But in private equity, CFOs often step into that role. It is about execution, planning, and navigating complexity."

And complexity came fast.

## Leading Through Disruption and Crisis

In early and mid-2025, Warrington continued to lead Beacon Wellness through some of the most challenging business conditions in memory. With 100% of sourcing in China, the company was facing global trade disruption, tariff uncertainty, and cash constraints. "It's a wartime CEO moment," she reflects. "But I've been through this before—during COVID at Wolverine—and I know how to manage through it."

She approached the challenge by meeting weekly with fellow portfolio company leaders, forecasting constantly, negotiating with factories, working with banks and legal teams, and maintaining proactive transparency with key partners like Walmart. “We didn’t wait,” she says. “We went to them early and honestly. That has been our best move so far,” she says as the challenges continue to affect the company.

## Top Five C-Suite Skills for the Future

When asked what skills will matter most for C-suite leaders in the years to come, Warrington offers five:

1. **Relationship Building and Trust:** “Even with difficult people, you need to find common ground. That is how I have succeeded—by learning what drives others and building mutual respect.”

2. **Flexibility and Agility:** “The pace of change is unlike anything we have seen. CEOs must pivot constantly, without losing focus.”

3. **Creative Problem-Solving:** “In our category, there is no playbook. Whether it is marketing restrictions or sourcing limits, we have to invent solutions.”

4. **Composure under Pressure:** “You may not feel calm inside, but you need to project calm. Teams take their cues from the CEO.”

5. **Perspective and Purpose:** "Family and health matter. That clarity helps you make better decisions at work."

## Burning Desire: Leading for the Next Generation

As she maintains her status in Beacon and watches her family grow, Maria's leadership lens extends beyond the business. Her burning desire? Preparing her children—and her team—for an unpredictable world.

"All I want is for my daughter to grow up and know how to manage challenging people," she says, only half-joking. "How do I help her build resilience, think critically, and face adversity with strength?"

This desire fuels both her personal life and her professional mission: to lead with intention, model courage, and guide others—through disruption, through ambiguity, and toward something better.

## Reflection

Maria Warrington's journey offers a clear lesson: Leadership is not about having all the answers—it is about finding a way forward. Her path from economic uncertainty to CEO demonstrates how introspection, persistence, and emotional intelligence shape not just career progression, but lasting impact. She reminds us that in the C-suite of the mid-2020s, adaptability is the strategy—and trust is the currency.

## **Bill Phillips: Strategy, Storytelling, and C-Suite Performance**

Bill Phillips is a seasoned media and health-care executive known for his innovative leadership in both publishing and digital health engagement.

Beginning in 2020, Bill served as the Chief Strategy and Performance Officer at Linkwell Health, a consumer engagement company that drives action in health care. In this role, he leverages more than 25 years of experience in behavior change expertise, audience-centric digital strategy, and leadership to enhance the company's performance and strategic direction.

Prior to his tenure at Linkwell Health, Bill spent 13 years at *Men's Health*, the world's largest men's magazine brand. As Vice President and Global Editor-in-Chief, he oversaw all aspects of the brand, both domestically and internationally. Under his leadership, Men's Health achieved significant milestones, including winning the National Magazine Award for General Excellence, the industry's highest honor.

Bill is also the author of the bestselling book *The Better Man Project* (Rodale Books), which offers more than 2,400 tips and techniques for men who want to improve various aspects of their lives, from health and fitness to mental well-being.

His career reflects a commitment to leveraging content and strategy to drive meaningful engagement and behavior change in both the media and health-care sectors.

"Strategy is a story: where we are, where we're going, and what's at stake if we don't move quickly."

## Editorial Clarity Meets Executive Intent

From the glossy pages of *Men's Health* to the operational corridors of Linkwell Health, Bill's career is a masterclass in clarity, agility, and purpose-driven leadership. As Global Editor-in-Chief, he shaped a media brand trusted by millions. As Chief Strategy and Performance Officer at Linkwell, he connects health-care consumers and vulnerable populations to the benefits, care, and clinical solutions they need to live their best lives.

**Pullout Insight:** Whether in publishing or population health, information quality and clarity are the foundations of trust.

"At *Men's Health*, we had a mantra: Make it actionable, make it evidence-based, and make it matter—now," Bill recalls. "I brought that same urgency to Linkwell. But instead of motivating readers to build abs, I'm now motivating health-care members and patients to better manage their blood sugar and show up for important screenings."

## Building Strategy Around Real Human Needs

Linkwell Health blends content, behavior change, and health-care outcomes. It is a place where strategy must drive both financial performance and human impact—a dual bottom line that comes with complexity.

"When I joined Linkwell, the biggest challenge was transforming a mission that mattered into a strategy that scaled," Bill says. "We had great people doing meaningful work, but our solutions, metrics, and momentum were not aligned. I had to work across silos to build a strategy road map that connected our purpose to our products and performance."

## The Hardest Challenge: Scaling Culture with Speed

As Linkwell grew rapidly—adding clients, expanding products, and building out data-driven personalization—Bill faced a classic C-suite dilemma: how to scale without breaking the soul of the business.

"The toughest challenge has not been technology or product-market fit. It's been infusing a performance-first mindset across the entire team."

He instituted new performance frameworks, defined clear success metrics, and helped leaders at every level shift from a reactive posture to a proactive, strategic mindset. Knowing what happened last week is great but winning in a competitive industry means being able to forecast next week's results accurately—and then delivering.

"I am not here to run meetings or build PowerPoints. My job is to build a connective tissue that links vision to execution. And sometimes that means hard conversations, prioritizing what we *do not* do and pulling the team back to the 'why.'"

## 5 Skills Every C-Suite Executive Needs

When asked what separates effective leaders from those who flame out in the C-suite, Bill offers five distinct skills:

1. **Narrative Intelligence:** The ability to craft, adapt, and communicate a compelling vision is nonnegotiable.

"If you can't tell the story behind your strategy, no one will follow."

2. **Cross-Functional Fluency:** Translation—not just delegation—is what builds alignment.

"You don't need to be an expert in every domain, but you need to speak the language of finance, tech, product, and people."

3. **Radical Prioritization:** Without ruthless prioritization, strategy dies in the fog of "nice to have."

"The C-suite is not about ideas—it is about choices. You have to say no to 100 good things to protect the three great ones."

4. **Emotional Stamina:** The human side of leadership often makes or breaks trust.

"You need a thicker skin and a softer heart. Feedback is constant. Pressure is real. You have to stay grounded, open, and consistent."

5. **Operational Curiosity:** A strategic plan without operational literacy is just a PowerPoint fantasy.

"Executives who stay curious about the 'how' avoid blind spots. You do not need to micromanage, but you must understand how execution happens."

## The CEO Is the Chief Clarity Officer

In a business environment filled with noise, data, and distraction, Bill believes the modern executive's job is simple but not easy.

"Our value is not in having the answers. It is in asking the right questions and getting everyone focused on the answers that matter."

He sees his role at Linkwell as more than driving performance. It is about building a company where people feel deeply connected to the mission and accountable for the outcomes.

## Final Thoughts: Leadership Is Emotional Work

Bill Phillips closes the conversation with a reflection that many C-suite leaders will find familiar:

"Leadership is emotional work. It is not just about insight; it is about presence. People do not remember your plan. They remember how you made them feel in the middle of the storm."

And that is what Bill tries to bring to every boardroom, every all-hands, every one-on-one: calm, conviction, and a clear sense of purpose.

You do not just need to manage the performance, he says. You need to perform the mission. That is what separates the good from the great in the C-suite.

## Amy Plasha: Adaptability, Authenticity, and a Focus on Talent

With over 30 years of experience in human resources, Amy Plasha has a proven track record of delivering effective leadership in all aspects of the field. As executive vice president and CHRO for Reworld Waste, which partners with businesses and communities to turn refuse into a resource, she leads the company's HR efforts, including compensation, benefits design and administration, talent acquisition, retention, organizational development, and change management.

Amy's goal is to align the company's people and culture with the business objectives. She works with a diverse group of people who possess a wide range of skills and expertise, and she brings them together by focusing on collaboration, agility, execution, leadership, and innovation.

Amy's expertise lies at the intersection of business strategy and people development. Her deep command of change management has enabled her to guide organizations through complex transformations, including mergers, acquisitions, and large-scale restructuring. At Reworld, she works to create a high-trust environment where employees and performance both thrive.

Amy is also a gifted executive coach and team-builder who cultivates resilient leadership teams. Her success stems from her technical skill and from an authentic ability to connect with people, ensuring that both the human and business sides of transformation are given equal weight.

## A Leadership Story of Growth, Alignment, and Resilience

When asked how she found her way to the C-suite, Amy humbly replies, "Truth be told, it was accidental." Her path was not a meticulously planned climb but a series of steps resulting from her willingness to say yes and the fortuitous presence of mentors who saw more in her than she saw in herself.

"I fell into HR by accident," she says in an interview. A temporary role in the human resources department became a gateway. From there, with each new opportunity, she leaned in. "If I had about 80% of what was needed, I'd raise my hand and figure out the other 20%." This growth mindset and courage to stretch became central to her career.

## Key Skill: Courageous Curiosity

Amy possesses an inquisitive nature, an openness to challenge, and the drive to learn beyond the job description. "I don't think I ever would have imagined myself at this level," she reflects.

Her pivotal moment came under the guidance of a leader who saw her potential and encouraged her to think more broadly. "[My] leader at the time played a pretty big role in that," she says. "Had we not had that conversation about what else I could do, I don't think I naturally would've gone that route."

## Key Skill: Influential Mentorship

The right mentor reframed her potential. It is a lesson she now pays forward. "You have to find someone who gives you that opportunity, who pushes and coaches you."

Her first true C-suite experience came at DBI, a private equity-backed company in turnaround. She was brought in as CHRO to build a strategic HR function from scratch.

"One day I was presenting to the board. Next, I was helping fill out I-9s at an acquisition. It was a humbling experience, but it taught me how to shift between tactical and strategic as necessary."

## Key Skill: Strategic Agility

Amy learned to operate fluidly between strategic leadership and tactical execution. "You have to shift, adapt, and meet people where they are," she says.

In later roles, she began to see the importance of aligning with the right leadership. "Cultural fit matters more than technical skill sometimes. I'd rather go without than bring in someone who doesn't align."

## Key Skill: Cultural Stewardship

Amy knows from experience that if the C-suite isn't aligned in how it leads, the leadership is ineffective. She learned that lesson the hard way in her most challenging position, at a previous company.

"What we said and how we acted were two different things," she remembers. The leadership team lacked alignment. "Some leaders were power-over, command-and-control, and I'm not that."

## Key Skill: Authenticity in Leadership

Amy stayed true to her values, even when it was uncomfortable. "I wasn't going to change how I lead to fit a style I didn't believe in," she says.

Eventually, she made the difficult decision to step away. "It was mutual. I needed to be with my family, and I could tell that the role was shifting."

In her role at Reworld she walked in with clarity. "There are three things I look for now: partnership with the CEO and the leadership team; ability to build and enhance the HR function; and alignment with the business's mission."

She learned from the Reworld CEO that empowerment matters. "I have never had a CEO say, 'I'll move the meeting time so you can spend more time with your family.' That's never happened before."

## Key Skill: Executive Collaboration

Her Reworld CEO sees her as a partner, not a function. That level of mutual respect allows her to focus on transformation.

Amy prioritizes talent strategy, providing early warning indicators to help identify issues and challenges before it's too late, and mergers and acquisitions integration. "Talent is everything," she says. "We're building out the next version of HR."

## Key Skill: Talent Magnetism

Amy understands the value of attracting and growing talent—and how the best leaders are talent developers. Developing leaders is essential to an organization because strong leadership drives performance, shapes culture, and ensures long-term sustainability. Effective leaders motivate teams, navigate change, and make strategic decisions that align with the company's vision. Leadership development also builds a pipeline of talent, reducing dependency on external hires and promoting internal growth. Investing in leaders fosters engagement and retention, creating a more resilient and adaptable organization.

## Key Skill: Integration Foresight

Having led numerous mergers and acquisitions, Amy knows how to shape the playbook. "We overlooked key aspects of recent acquisitions—particularly talent assessment and integration. That's precisely where I can add value."

## Final Reflections

Looking at the leadership environment, Amy emphasizes a few skills critical for C-suite success:

- **Cross-Functional Fluency:** "You can't just stay in your lane. You have to understand the whole business and partner effectively with those who can help provide greater understanding."

- **Tech Adaptability:** "Leverage AI and tools. Work smarter, not harder."
- **Data-Driven Decision Making:** "Data removes emotion from decisions."

Amy's journey is marked by adaptability, clarity, and principle. She concludes, "Looking back on this..., I felt so well-prepared walking into this new role—calm, even-keeled."

Her experience is a living example of what happens when leaders lead with courage, empathy, and vision—and why those who truly *start leading, stop managing* thrive in today's C-suite.

## Jacob Ross: Don't Follow Someone Else's Path, Shape Your Own

Jacob Ross did not take the standard route to the CEO seat, and that is precisely why his story is important.

Growing up just outside Dartmouth College in Vermont, Jacob learned early what resilience and reinvention look like. His father worked at the same hospital for over forty years. His mother, on the other hand, took a bold leap, returning to school in her 50s to become a psychotherapist. That decision left a deep impression on Jacob. "It taught me that your trajectory is something you can shape," Jacob says. "There's no straight line unless you draw it."

At Reed College in Portland, Oregon, Jacob dove into Russian literature—not for the grades (which the school famously does not prioritize), but for the critical thinking, exploration, and edge-of-the-map curiosity the interest fostered. He followed that curiosity to Tokyo and St. Petersburg, experiences that broadened his worldview and stretched his appetite for risk. So, naturally, he moved to Wall Street.

"I wanted the opposite of everything I'd known," he says. "I crashed on a friend's floor and landed a $29,000-a-year job at a trading firm. I felt like I had made it."

## Finding the Right Fit

But ambition does not sit still for long. After stints at Bloomberg and Right Media, Jacob found his calling in the fast-moving world of ad tech. "That's where I met my people—builders, dreamers, challengers of the status quo," he says. It was also where he began refining the leadership muscle that would carry him to the top.

He ran ad platforms at Demand Media, led North America at Criteo, and stepped into the Chief Product Officer role at MediaMath. At each of his jobs, Jacob did not just climb ladders—he built bridges. Each role was a masterclass in scale, speed, and reinvention. However, his biggest shift came not from changing industries, but from changing his mindset.

"You have to move beyond your functional expertise," he explains. "Leadership means you stop thinking only like a specialist and start acting like a business owner."

That mindset brought him to the marketing company PebblePost, first as President and then as CEO during a COVID-era transformation. At PebblePost, he saw a chance to pioneer a new category: Programmatic Direct Mail powered by real-time intent data. "We went from survival to growth," Jacob says. "And I've never been more fulfilled."

## Culture of Performance

Ask Jacob what drives him, and his answer is clear: "Realizing the vision." But he is quick to add that it's not just about the product.

"It's about building a high-performance culture where the right people can do the best work of their careers."

That clarity shows up in how he leads. Jacob demands boldness and accountability from his team. "Call your shot. Deliver. Do not spend a year chasing 2% gains, make it matter." He also prizes smart brevity, insisting that clarity and impact go hand in hand.

Jacob's expectations for leaders are refreshingly blunt: "I want business leaders who happen to have functional expertise, not functional experts pretending to be business leaders."

## Urgency Without Chaos

He is equally pragmatic about time. "We are a time-boxed experiment. Tech companies do not have infinite runways. The challenge is creating urgency without creating chaos." And while his gaze is always forward, Jacob makes time to sharpen his edge. As a member of the 10x CEO community, he surrounds himself with peers who challenge him. "It's like having a second board," he says. "Peer learning is the most underrated growth tool for CEOs."

One area he is pushing hard is AI. "This is not just a wave. It is a paradigm shift, bigger than cloud. If we do not embrace it, we risk becoming irrelevant."

## Leadership Lessons from Jacob Ross

- **Shape Your Own Path:** Reinvention is not an exception; it is a strategy.

- **Move from Expert to Owner:** Stop optimizing the function. Start owning the business.
- **Be Outcome-Oriented:** Bold goals and accountability win over incrementalism.
- **Communicate With Clarity:** Smart brevity beats corporate jargon.
- **Learn with Peers:** No one grows in isolation. Your network is your edge.
- **Lead With Urgency, Not Chaos:** The clock is ticking. Make it count without burning out your team.

Jacob Ross didn't inherit a map to the top, he carved one himself, guided by risk, reinvention, and relentless vision. The path wasn't without pain, however, and the scars he carries are proof that real growth comes not from easy wins but from hard-won lessons.

# 9

# Leaders I Have Admired Over the Years

Over the course of my career, I have been fortunate to work with and learn from exceptional leaders across a variety of industries. Each one shaped how I think about leadership: what works, what doesn't, and most importantly, what endures. These individuals taught me lessons that continue to influence how I lead today.

## Richard Darwick

Richard Darwick was my first real boss. As co-director of Pine Brook Day Camp, he gave me my first opportunity as a counselor-in-training (CIT) at the age of 12. That summer marked the beginning of a 12-year journey working under Richard's guidance, earning new responsibilities year after year.

A former New York City school executive, Richard was brilliant, respected, and decisive. He had a strong presence, a keen sense of street smarts, and a deep understanding of how to connect with kids. More than anything, he taught me the importance of building relationships, showing genuine care, and setting clear boundaries—lessons that have stayed with me ever since.

**Richard taught me that leading begins with caring, and that strong relationships are the foundation of effective leadership.**

## Jack Welch

Five months after Jack Welch became CEO of General Electric, I joined the company fresh out of Columbia University as part of the prestigious Global Human Resources Program. At the time, GE was 80% manufacturing and 20% services. By the time I left, that mix had reversed.

Jack's transformation of GE was nothing short of remarkable. He was a no-nonsense leader with a clear and compelling vision. He surrounded himself with tough-minded, performance-driven executives in his own mold. While his style delivered results, it also came at a human cost. Welch taught me the power of bold vision and the importance—and consequences—of relentless execution.

**From Jack, I learned that strong leadership demands vision and courage—but also awareness of the human toll it may take.**

## Ed Meagher

At PepsiCo, Ed Meagher managed the KFC business on the East Coast during the critical period when Pepsi had acquired Taco Bell, Pizza Hut, and KFC. Ed embodied what it meant to lead rather than manage. He challenged our team to think strategically, elevate the customer experience, and invest in operational excellence. Under his leadership, I learned how to see beyond the day-to-day and lead with a long-term perspective.

**Ed reminded me that leadership is about seeing the bigger picture and inspiring others to move toward it.**

## Don Supina

When I started at GE, my first assignment placed me at a manufacturing facility in Holland, Michigan, where, as a corporate program hire, I was not exactly welcomed with open arms. Locals saw me as "corporate overhead," someone they had not asked for. That changed when Don Supinacame in as the new head of HR following a divisional merger. Don gave me real responsibilities, trusted me to build relationships with staff and line workers, and treated me as a valued member of the team. That trust made all the difference, and it laid the foundation for a successful career at GE.

**Don taught me that trust is a powerful tool—and often the first step in turning potential into performance.**

## Dick Hernandez

Dick Hernandez served as CEO during a challenging merger between IBM and Kodak's services businesses. He had spent over two decades at IBM, and while he was supportive of my role—tasked with building a new culture for the combined entity—the effort ultimately proved untenable.

Legacy cultures run deep, and the leadership team remained primarily composed of IBM and Kodak veterans. I learned a difficult but necessary lesson: Even with executive support, cultural transformation is impossible without structural alignment and shared commitment. Hernandez did his best to back me, and I have always respected him for that.

**Dick helped me understand that even strong leadership can be limited by systems, structure, and history.**

## Steve Murphy

At Rodale Inc., a family-owned publishing company focused on healthy living, I was asked to recruit a new CEO as the Rodale family sought to scale the business. We brought in Steve Murphy from Disney, and under his leadership, the company grew from $250 million to over $700 million in eight years. Murphy was a master at talent assessment, brand innovation, and scaling through multiple revenue streams. He transformed the organization by building contemporary brands like *Women's Health* and by fostering a culture of excellence, accountability, and creative thinking.

**Steve showed me that growth comes not just from ambition, but from aligning talent, vision, and innovation.**

## Kass and Mike Lazerow

Kass and Mike Lazerow are entrepreneurs in the truest sense of the word. They built Buddy Media and sold it to Salesforce for $750 million. What impressed me most was not just their business success but their integrity. They led with open minds, grounded values, and a genuine respect for the people they worked with.

The husband-and-wife team made decisions with purpose and principle, never asking their team to do something they would not do themselves. Their humility and humanity remain rare qualities in the business world, and I continue to admire them deeply.

**Kass and Mike taught me that authentic leadership is rooted in humility, values, and empathy.**

# 10

# References


Center for Creative Leadership. (March 4, 2025). *The leadership gap: how to fix what your organization lacks.* https://www.ccl.org/articles/leading-effectively-articles/leadership-gap-what-you-still-need

Dewar, C., Hirt, M., and Keller, S. (October 2019). *The mindsets and practices of excellent CEOs.* McKinsey & Company. https://www.mckinsey.com/~/media/McKinsey/Business%20Functions/Strategy%20and%20Corporate%20Finance/Our%20Insights/The%20mindsets%20and%20practices%20of%20excellent%20CEOs/The-mindsets-and-practices-of-excellent-CEOs_F.pdfhttps://www.mckinsey.com/~/media/McKinsey/Business%20Functions/Strategy%20and%20Corporate%20Finance/Our%20Insights/The%20mindsets%20and%20practices%20of%20excellent%20CEOs/The-mindsets-and-practices-of-excellent-CEOs_F.pdf

Goleman, D. (2017). *What makes a leader.* Harvard Business Review.

Ou, A.Y., Tsui, A.S., Kinicki, A.J., Waldman, D.A., Xiao, Z., & Song, L.J. (2014). Humble chief executive officers' connections to top management team integration and middle managers' responses. Administrative Science Quarterly, 59(1), 34–72. https://doi.org/10.1177/0001839213520131

Phillips, B. (2015). *The Better Man Project: 2,476 tips and techniques that will flatten your belly, sharpen your mind, and keep you healthy and happy for life!* Rodale Books.

*PwC 2021 Annual Corporate Directors Survey*. (October 2021). PricewaterhouseCoopers LLP (PwC US), Governance Insights Center. https://www.corporatecomplianceinsights.com/wp-content/uploads/2021/10/pwc-2021-annual-corporate-directors-survey.pdf

Scott, K. (March 14, 2017). *Radical candor: Be a kick-ass boss without losing your humanity*. St. Martin's Press.

*Workplace conflict and how businesses can harness it to thrive*. (2008). CPP Global Human Capital Report. https://shop.themyersbriggs.com/Pdfs/CPP_Global_Human_Capital_Report_Workplace_Conflict.pdf

Willink, J. (November 21, 2017). *Extreme ownership: how U.S. Navy SEALS lead and win*. St. Martin's Press.

# About the Author

Michael Bruno is a seasoned executive and leadership advisor with over 30 years of experience driving organizational transformation across human resources, operations, and corporate strategy. He is a partner at TKJ Leadership, a boutique firm specializing in executive search, executive coaching, organizational effectiveness, and talent assessment.

Previously, Michael served as founder and CEO of New Directions for Grads (ND4G), a progressive executive search and advisory firm known for building world-class management teams and delivering transformative leadership solutions.

Throughout his career, Michael has held senior leadership roles at companies such as GE, PepsiCo, IBM, Interactive Corp. (IAC), and Buddy Media (acquired by Salesforce). He also has partnered with prominent private equity firms including Sterling Partners, Angelo Gordon, and Centerbridge Partners.

His work has contributed to organizations earning distinctions such as Fortune's 100 Best Companies to Work For and Most Admired Company.

**Get Your Book Bonuses**

**Scan to Access**

Made in the USA
Monee, IL
04 November 2026

67382342R00144